The Canadian's Guide to Stock Investing

Updated Edition

by Andrew Dagys, CPA, CMA, and
Paul Mladjenovic, CFP

WILEY

Publisher's Acknowledgments

Authors:
Andrew Dagys, CPA, CMA, and Paul Mladjenovic, CFP

Senior Acquisitions Editor: Tracy Boggier

Project Manager: Susan Pink

Compilation Editor: Georgette Beatty

Production Editor: Saikarthick Kumarasamy

Cover Photo: © muhamad rukmana/ Getty Images

The Canadian's Guide to Stock Investing, Updated Edition

Published by John Wiley & Sons, Inc.
111 River St.
Hoboken, NJ 07030-5774
`http://www.wiley.com`

For general information on our other products and services, please contact our Business Development Department in the U.S. at 317-572-3205.

Library of Congress Control Number: 2022935355

ISBN 978-1-119-89270-0 (pbk)

SKY10033813_061422

Table of Contents

1

Your Financial Goals

Yes, you want to make the big bucks. Or maybe you just want to get back the big bucks you lost in stocks during *a recent market correction* (a short period of falling prices usually accompanied by lots of volatility). Either way, you want your money to grow so that you can have a better life.

But before you make reservations for that Caribbean cruise you're dreaming about, you have to map out your action plan to get there. Investing in stocks can be a great component of most wealth-building programs, but you must first do some homework on a topic that you should be very familiar with — yourself. That's right. More than ever before, you need to understand your current financial situation and clearly define your financial goals as the first steps to successful and careful investing.

Here's an example. Steve had a million dollars' worth of Procter & Gamble (PG) stock and was nearing retirement. Steve wondered about selling this stock and becoming more growth-oriented by investing in a batch of *small cap* stocks (stocks of a company worth $300 million to $2 billion). Because Steve already had enough assets to retire on at that time, getting more aggressive wasn't necessary. In fact, Steve had too much tied to a single stock, even though it was a solid, large company. What would happen to Steve's assets if problems arose at PG?

A diversified stock portfolio should include multiple stocks (more than 20) from various sectors and countries. Shrinking his stock portfolio and putting that money elsewhere — by paying off debt, adding a guaranteed investment certificate (GIC) from a Canadian bank, or buying a U.S. Treasury bill (a fixed-income security) for diversification, for example — seemed obvious.

This chapter is undoubtedly one of the most important chapters in this book. At first, you may think it's a chapter more suitable for some general book on personal finance. Wrong! The greatest weakness of unsuccessful investors is not understanding their financial situations and how stocks fit in.

People should stay out of the stock market if they aren't prepared for the responsibilities of stock investing, such as regularly reviewing corporate financial statements and the progress of the companies they invest in.

Investing in stocks requires balance. Investors sometimes tie up too much money in stocks, putting themselves at risk of losing a significant portion of their wealth if the market plunges. This approach is especially dangerous for the many Canadians who hold on to excessive personal debt, which has been rising nationally over the years. Then again, other Canadian investors place little or no money in stocks and therefore miss out on excellent opportunities to meaningfully grow their wealth and keep up with inflation.

TIP

Canadians should make stocks a part of their investment portfolios, but the operative word is *part*. Most investors hold a balanced portfolio, composed of stocks, bonds, and other financial assets. You should let stocks take up only a *portion* of your money. A disciplined investor also has money in bank accounts, investment-grade bonds, precious metals, and other assets that offer growth or income opportunities. Diversification is the key to minimizing risk. (For more on risk, see Chapter 3.)

Different Types of Financial Goals

Consider stocks as tools for living, just like any other investment — no more, no less. Stocks are among the many tools you use to accomplish something — to achieve a goal. Yes, successfully investing in stocks is the goal that you're probably shooting for because you're reading this book. However, you must complete the following sentence: "I want to be successful in my stock investing program to accomplish _____." You must consider stock investing as a means to an end.

Know the difference between long-term, intermediate-term, and short-term goals, and then set some of each (see Chapter 2 for more information):

- *Long-term goals* refer to projects or financial goals that need funding more than ten years from now.
- *Intermediate-term goals* refer to financial goals that need funding five to ten years from now.
- *Short-term* goals need funding less than five years from now.

Stocks, in general, are best suited for long-term goals such as achieving financial independence (think retirement funding), paying for future college or university costs, or paying for any long-term expenditure or project.

Some categories of stock (such as conservative or large cap) may be suitable for intermediate-term financial goals. If, for example, you'll retire six years from now, conservative stocks combined with some quality fixed-income investments can be appropriate. If you're optimistic *(bullish)* about the stock market and confident that stock prices will rise, go ahead and invest. However, if you're negative about the market *(bearish)* and believe that stock prices will decline, you may want to wait until the economy starts to forge a clear path. To explore some exciting and emerging megatrends, sectors, and industries within sectors, flip to Chapter 6.

TIP

In recent years, investors have sought quick, short-term profits by trading and speculating in stocks. Lured by the fantastic returns generated by the stock market in the original dot-com and internet 2.0 eras (about when Meta Platforms and Alphabet, formerly known as Facebook and Google respectively, came to town) investors saw stocks as a get-rich-quick scheme. Understanding the differences among *investing, saving,* and *speculating* is important. Which one do you want to do? Knowing the answer to this question is crucial to your goals and aspirations. Investors who don't know the differences tend to get burned. The following will help you distinguish among these actions:

- ***Investing* is the act of putting your current funds into securities or tangible assets to gain future**

appreciation, income, or both. You need time, knowledge, and discipline to invest. The investment can fluctuate in price but has been chosen for long-term potential.

- ***Saving* is the safe accumulation of funds for a future use.** Savings don't fluctuate and are generally free of financial risk. The emphasis is on safety and liquidity.
- ***Speculating* is the financial world's equivalent of gambling.** An investor who speculates is seeking quick profits gained from short-term price movements in a particular asset or investment. In recent years, many folks have been trading stocks (buying and selling in the short term with frequency), which is in the realm of short-term speculating.

These distinctly different concepts are often confused, even among so-called financial experts.

Canadians in Their 20s and 30s: How to Set the Foundation

One key piece of stock investing is understanding how your age will influence your stock-investing decisions.

Canadians in their 20s and 30s are a logical place to begin. This cohort enjoys a tremendous luxury in addition to being young — they have a long-term time frame before retirement comes into the picture. If you're young, the amount of funds you can allocate to stock investing is a lot greater than if you are an older Canadian. That's because you can ride any stock market corrections and storms that will come along from time to time. In fact, stock market turbulence creates an ideal opportunity to buy low and sell high, or just buy low and hold for now. The younger you are, the more opportunities you have to rinse and repeat this dynamic process. That's a lot better than ending up at the cleaners.

Another luxury a young Canadian stock investor can enjoy is the development of a mindset with a focus on investment planning, a critical success factor in stock investing. *Planning* in this case means taking the time to master the fundamentals of stock investing and to learn from mistakes. If you do so, the invariable hiccups and slumps in stock prices won't jeopardize your entire stock portfolio because you will have a longer time frame to recoup any losses and a more confident and less fearful mindset. As long as you embrace the reality, opportunity, and risks presented by stock market volatility, this is the time in life to invest a bit more aggressively.

With a better understanding of your net assets, cash inflows and outflows, and personal goals and investment return expectations, you're poised to make better sense of your investing options. These options include equities as well as bonds, real estate, and other areas you can park your hard-earned cash into. The younger you are, the more risk you can tolerate and the more compounding of returns you can take advantage of. This is where you begin the even more fun part of your stock-investing journey.

Determine the right allocation to stocks and other equities

Whatever age you may be, most of the principles in this book will apply. In other words, this book is age-agnostic. However, one important exception is how age relates to your risk tolerance and appetite and therefore how much you devote to stocks.

TIP One key concept is simple: the younger you are — say, in your 20s and 30s — the more risk you can afford to take on. In fact, *failure* to seize an opportunity to make outsized returns, due especially to the power of compounding and reinvested returns, is itself a risk. Inflation is also an enemy because it can quickly eat up cash savings.

This section outlines some general guidelines for optimal equity-asset allocations relative to your young age. It introduces the concepts of passive and aggressive investing, and taxation, although you'll hear more about those things in later chapters as well.

To be sure, stocks are riskier than bonds, but that's over shorter time frames, when you're likely to run into significant price volatility. Long-term history shows time and again that dips in the stock market are invariably made up after some time passes.

A prevailing view, and these are just judgement calls, is that Canadians in their 20s and 30s should have about 70 percent in equities and the balance in fixed-income investments such as bonds. If this is held in a tax-free savings account, or TFSA, the ratio in equities could be even higher. TFSAs in the context of stock investing are introduced in the next section.

Because younger Canadians can afford, time-wise, to take a more aggressive and less risk-averse stance on stocks, they're more prone to look for growth stocks and stories. They're likely, even more than older investors, to be familiar with stocks of growing technology companies such as Twitter, Amazon, Spotify, and Apple. However, anyone in this age cohort shouldn't put an excessive amount of money into one particular area, such as going all-in for growth stocks, which is a category known for high volatility. In other words, it's important to diversify, especially if you're just learning the stock-investing ropes.

When it comes to choosing one type of equity instrument over another, equity mutual funds aren't a great choice as compared to stocks or ETFs (exchange-traded funds). Mutual funds do not typically generate high growth. They also come with higher and often hidden fees that eat into your returns. They're more expensive than ETFs. Although they're less volatile during downturns, they often defeat the purpose of growth investing. Equity ETFs, on the other hand, at least offer you better growth prospects. Equity mutual funds may bury you in a sea of fees and offer you low-end returns.

Start off by investing in big picture themes

The Internet of Things. Cannabis and marijuana. Electric vehicles. Stock markets in China and the rest of Asia. Even the blockchain. These are but a few of the exciting and innovative themes, concepts, and stories that drive investment headlines worldwide today. Handled properly, stock investing in these areas can provide equally exciting returns. Chapter 6 provides you with insights on how to seize investment opportunities in some of these new domains. It also discusses even more traditional but continuously growing sectors and industries, such as healthcare, travel, real estate, and resources.

But if you're in your 20s or 30s, your most significant investments likely to compete with and complement stock investing are investments in real estate and your education, including educating yourself in stock investing.

Home sweet home

In much the same way that equity investing does not have to be restricted to pure stock investing, what with the availability of alternatives such as equity ETFs and mutual funds, real estate investing can vary as well.

For example, you might invest in a home, condominium, or commercial or residential investment property. Yet once again, the stock market offers alternatives to even these traditional investment opportunities. Real estate investment trusts (REITs) are traded on Canadian and U.S. stock exchanges and relate to all types of real estate — malls, apartments, offices, and even prisons. With the current frothy and often inaccessible Canadian real estate market, especially in cities such as Toronto and Vancouver, it can make good personal and financial sense to still be in the game. You can achieve this by investing in property through the REIT option.

As you can see, the stock market has something for everyone. But it has to be navigated carefully, and this book provides you with a compass to traverse the market's choppy waters.

Education and personal development

Perhaps the most important investment is the investment you make in your education. The best annuity in the world is one powered and inspired by the knowledge you build in your head and intellect.

This book contains proven, tried, and tested investing and financial fundamentals. You won't be disappointed, no matter what your current knowledge level is. Your 20s and 30s are an ideal time to get that knowledge.

Your tax-free savings account (TFSA) as a tax-free stock investing account

One tax-smart strategy needs a basic introduction. It's the *tax-free savings account*, or *TFSA*. The TFSA was designed by the government with stocks top of mind. TFSAs are presented here in the context of age because the more time and risk appetite you have to invest in stocks, the more conducive a TFSA will be to your investment portfolio structure.

You may invest not only in stocks but also in guaranteed investment certificates (GICs), bonds, mutual funds, simple cash, and more. The key tax and total return advantage is that a TFSA allows you to invest in eligible investments and lets those savings grow tax free throughout your lifetime. For example, dividends, capital gains, and interest earned in a TFSA are tax free for life. You can take out your accumulated TFSA savings from your account at any time, and for any reason. This tax-free growth also means that all withdrawals are tax free.

Although you can save for any personal goal you want (such as a new car, home, or vacation), TFSAs are ideal for *growth* stocks. Stocks grow in two key ways: by capital gains (if the stock value rises) and by dividends (assuming the stock you hold in the tax-free account pays dividends).

TIP

Whether you're just beginning to build your financial portfolio or just placing all your savings in a TFSA as you begin to pay off your new mortgage, credit card, auto loan, or student loans, just note that you have two stock-allocation decisions:

- How much of your overall net investable cash do you want to allocate to stocks and other equities?
- Do you want this allocation to be inside or outside of a tax-smart savings account such as a TFSA?

Invest in your company registered pension or retirement savings plan

Young Canadians should consider registered pension plans. These tax and savings plans are primarily your *registered retirement savings plan (RRSP)* as well as your company registered pension plan (if offered by your employer). Most Canadians strive to make or match employer contributions into one or both of these savings vehicles. So, in addition to TFSAs, be mindful of these latter plans as you consider your total portfolio and percentage allocation to stocks. Like TFSAs, RRSPs and employer pension plans exist to help to set you up for a stable financial future. For more on retirement planning, see the *Canadian's Guide to Retirement Planning* (Wiley).

Canadian Stock Investors in Their 40s

If you're in the 40+ age bracket, you're in or are approaching your peak earning years and are likely reducing personal debt. As a result, you may have a bit more to sock away into stocks. If that's not your reality, this is the ideal time to take stock investing seriously. You still have plenty of time to take advantage of the potential for much better growth than bonds or just plain old cash can offer. This assumes you have embraced a longer-term mindset, which is a luxury you can still have in your 40s.

This section explores reasonable allocations to stocks, as well as potential tax and pension options and strategies you should be aware of.

Common investment portfolio allocations to stocks

As Canadian stock investors get older, the asset-allocation equation typically begins to shift toward fixed investments such as bonds. However, this recalibration over time still depends on your existing risk tolerance or appetite, and that in turn is driven by your goals and financial plans and needs.

If you're in your 40s and consider yourself to be risk averse — a deeper discussion of conservative, aggressive, and other approaches to stock investing follows in Chapter 2 — you may be comfortable with a 50 to 60 percent stock and 50 to 40 percent bond allocation range. If you're a more aggressive investor in this age bracket, you may very well be at ease with a 70 to 80 percent stock allocation, if not more.

Yet another perspective is time to retirement. If you have 25 years to retire, 85 percent can be in stocks; if you have 15 years to retire, that figure for stocks versus bonds goes down to about 70 percent. In a low-interest-rate environment, where your potential for outsized fixed-income returns is limited, a reasonable rule of thumb promoted by the investment industry is that you should invest 75 percent of your assets in stocks and 25 percent in bonds in your 40s. Whenever interest rates rise, as they have been lately, adjust that ratio accordingly.

The point of these examples or conventions is much more substantive — your allocation depends on several variables over and above just age. These additional variables include risk tolerance, interest rates, market conditions, and investor acumen, something you'll sharpen as you read this book. Another key point is that the more assets you allocate to stock holdings, the more volatile your stock-investing experience will be, both on the upside and on the downside.

Always keep in mind that investment diversification — which is really risk mitigation or risk management — is not just a binary stock-versus-bond equation or debate. As you discover in this book, you can exploit many shades of grey. As mentioned, equities include not just stocks but also exchange-traded funds and real estate investment trusts. Diversify even more deeply, still within equities per se, by holding not just domestic stocks, ETFs, and REITs but also international equivalents. You must absolutely know about these lower-fee and easy-to-trade ETF and REIT alternatives, which are great ways to keep more money in your hands rather than in the hands of sometimes expensive fund managers or inexperienced financial advisors.

Taxes, company pensions, and registered retirement savings plans (RRSPs)

It's always a good idea to park as much as you can in a pension plan, but that's a lot easier said than done. Competing priorities and associated costs related to marriage, buying a home, travel, healthcare, and just plain old living life stand in the way of pension planning. Yet, for many Canadians in their 40s, this is the exact time when some extra cash can be found. Perhaps a raise, a bequest, or a seriously dented mortgage balance has found its way to you. If so, you may find yourself in a great position to invest in an existing or a new pension plan, and — as importantly — to make stocks a key part of that plan.

If you're lucky, you have a company pension plan that invests on your behalf, likely in lots of stocks. If you are really lucky, that pension plan is of the *defined benefit* variety. Even with such a plan, consider investing more within a registered retirement saving plan, or RRSP. We cover RRSPs and the tax implications and fun new rules (okay, they're not really fun) in Chapter 8.

TIP: The key message is that if you have not yet saved in your employer's pension plan or don't have that option, start thinking about RRSPs now.

RRSPs are a future-oriented "forced" savings vehicle with a tax structure that benefits you (you get a deduction in high tax-bracket years and are taxed on RRSP withdrawals in later and lower tax-bracket retirement years). In contrast, TFSAs are more mid-range in terms of planning horizons. Within RRSPs, and as your stock-investing expertise and comfort grows, you can look at more company- and industry-specific stocks and away from themes.

50-Something Canadian Stock Investors

As Canadians move into their 50s, stock-investing decisions should be geared towards safer stocks (that is, ones that are financially stable, and less cyclical and volatile) and dividend-paying stocks.

Canadians who are 50-plus and 60-plus years old may still be in their peak earning years. But as far as their investment time horizon is concerned, their peak investing years are behind them. At the same time, though, what with the average life expectancy in Canada pushing into the mid-80s, Canadian stock investors still need to consider their investment portfolios. Sitting still can be hazardous to financial health. The goal in your late 50s and 60s is to have an investment portfolio that will sustain you throughout your retirement years.

TIP

If you are in your 60s, you want to calibrate your portfolio away from stocks and more toward an income stream. But recall what was said in the previous section, namely, that equities come in different shapes, sizes, and, more importantly, risk profiles. You can lower your stock-investing risk and still stay in stocks by considering exchange-traded funds as well as real estate investment trusts. In your 50+ years, don't just hold domestic equities — consider some stable international equities as well. Dividend-paying stocks and international stock investing are extremely important for 50+ investors.

Revisit your allocation to stocks

The 50+ age zone is the time to examine your retirement goals and desired retirement lifestyle. You can't do that in a vacuum. Consider your existing income flows, projected income streams, and your tax situation, including special tax rules for older Canadians. Just because you're older is not a reason to take your foot off the investing accelerator. Rather, it's more of a time to pay special attention to hazard signs. You've learned a lot about investing by this time, so you don't have to throw that knowledge away. Warren Buffett doesn't. Even if you're older and are new to stock investing, growth is still a consideration. Equities are still a very real alternative.

TIP

A typical rule of thumb for those in their 50s and 60s is to have about half of your portfolio in conservative equities and the rest in fixed-income financial instruments such as bonds. Note that *equities* refer to stocks, ETFs, and equity mutual funds. Also recall that if, for example, you have 15 years to retirement, one of several rules of thumb is that the ratio of equities versus bonds can be 70 percent. No golden year rule exists.

If you're a savvy and careful stock investor, you may want to invest as much as 75 percent in equities and 25 percent in fixed-income financial instruments, again depending on other variables already mentioned in this chapter. Decades ago, a half-and-half ratio of equities to bonds was reasonable and effective. That's when interest rates were high and heavily rewarded savers. Today, interest-rates are lower, so finding significant, guaranteed fixed-income returns is difficult.

A final variable to consider when determining your investment allocation to stocks is the nature, extent, and timing of your withdrawal of investment resources. What will you sell first — your house, cottage, or other assets? Will you continue to work part-time past your retirement age? In addition, when do you expect to draw from your Canadian government entitlements such as Canada Pension Plan (CPP) or Old Age Security (OAS)? This is where tax-planning and stock-investing decisions have to be integrated — topics that are beyond the scope of this book. These more complex considerations will also drive your decisions regarding allocations to stocks at this stage of life.

TIP

For all stock-allocation decisions for all stages of life, don't just look at one investment or savings account in isolation. Be mindful of your big picture. Look at your entire investment portfolio. Consider company pensions, RRSPs, TFSAs, and government retirement annuities you're entitled to. As one Canadian bank commercial reminds us: "You may be richer than you think!" If so, you can continue to delve into the exciting and potentially rewarding realm of stock investing, with an even greater allocation.

Taxes, registered pensions, and registered retirement income funds (RRIFs)

If you're over 50, note the importance of taxes and financial planning. Although extreme tax planning is beyond the intent of this book, the relevant (stock-investing) basics of Canadian taxation appear in Chapter 8.

Registered retirement income funds (RRIFs) allow you to withdraw some of your registered savings in a tax-smart way.

As for other retirement-planning decisions regarding estate planning, income splitting, foreign taxes, and the use of TFSAs versus RRSPs to park your money, you should seek the specialized expertise of a qualified professional. But if you have a simpler portfolio, see Chapter 4, which introduces you to the latest innovation in financial technology, called *robo-advisors*.

2

Common Approaches to Stock Investing

"Investing for the long term" isn't just some perfunctory investment slogan. It's a culmination of proven stock market experience that goes back many decades. Unfortunately, investor buying and selling habits have deteriorated in recent years due to impatience. Today's investors think that the short term is measured in days, the intermediate term is measured in weeks, and the long term is measured in months. Yeesh! No wonder so many Canadians are complaining about lousy investment returns. Investors have lost the profitable art of patience.

What should you do? Become an investor with a time horizon greater than one year (the emphasis is on *greater*). Give your investments time to grow. Everybody dreams about emulating the success of someone like Warren Buffett, but few emulate his patience, which is a huge part of his investment success.

Stocks are tools you can use to build your wealth. When used wisely, for the right purpose and in the right environment, they do a great job. But when improperly applied, they can lead to disaster. This chapter shows you how to choose the right types of investments based on your short-term, intermediate-term, and long-term financial goals. It also shows you how to decide on your purpose for investing (growth or income investing) and your style of investing (conservative or aggressive).

How to Invest for the Future

Individual stocks can be either great or horrible choices, depending on the time period you want to focus on. Generally, you can plan to invest in stocks for the short, intermediate, or long term. These sections outline which stocks are most appropriate for each term length.

Investing in quality stocks becomes less risky as the time frame lengthens. Stock prices tend to fluctuate daily and trend up or down over an extended period of time. Even if you invest in a stock that goes down in the short term, you're likely to see it rise and possibly exceed your investment if you have the patience to wait it out and let the stock price appreciate.

The short term

Short term generally means five years or less. Short-term investing isn't about making a quick buck — it refers to when you may need the money. Every person has short-term goals. Some are modest, such as setting aside money for a vacation next month or paying for medical bills. Other short-term goals are more ambitious, such as accruing funds for a down payment to purchase a new home in downtown Winnipeg within six months. Whatever the expense or purchase, you need a predictable accumulation of cash soon. If this sounds like your situation, stay away from the stock market.

TIP

Because stocks can be so unpredictable in the short term, they're a bad choice for short-term considerations. You may hear market analysts on TV saying things such as, "At $25 a share, XYZ is a solid investment, and we feel that its stock should hit our target price of $40 within six to nine months." You know that an eager investor hears that and says, "Gee, why bother with 1 percent at the bank when this stock will rise by more than 50 percent? I'd better place a trade through an online broker." It may hit that target amount (or surpass it), or it may not. Most of the time, the stock doesn't reach the target price, and the investor is disappointed. The stock can even go down. Do not rely on analyst forecasts. (Online brokers are covered in Chapter 4.)

The reason that target prices are frequently missed is because figuring out what millions of investors will do in the short term is difficult. The short term can be irrational because so many investors have so many reasons for buying and selling that it can be difficult to analyze. If you invest for an important short-term need, you can lose very important cash quicker than you think.

During the recent bull market, Canadian investors watched as some high-profile stocks, especially U.S. stocks, went up 20 to 50 percent in a matter of months. Hey, who needs a savings account earning a measly interest rate when stocks grow like that? Of course, when a bear market eventually "opens for business" — and it always does — those same stocks may very well see 50 to 70 percent price drops, as we also witnessed recently. A savings account earning a measly interest rate from a bank suddenly wouldn't seem so bad.

Short-term stock investing is unpredictable. Stocks — even the best ones — fluctuate in the short term. In a negative environment, they can be volatile. No one can accurately predict the price movement (unless you has some inside information). You can better serve your short-term goals with stable, interest-bearing investments such as guaranteed investment certificates (GICs) at your bank.

Intermediate-term goals

Intermediate term refers to the financial goals you plan to reach in five to ten years. For example, if you want to accumulate funds to put money down for investment in real estate six years from now, some growth-oriented investments may be suitable. (Growth investing is discussed in more detail later in this chapter.)

Although some stocks may be appropriate for a two- or three-year period as part of a larger balanced portfolio, not all stocks are good intermediate-term investments. Some stocks are fairly stable and hold their value well, such as the stock of large or established dividend-paying companies. Canadian bank, pipeline, and utility stocks come to mind. Other stocks have prices that jump all over the place, such as those of untested companies that haven't been in existence long enough to develop a consistent track record. Junior mining and technology stocks such as blockchain (bitcoin-related) stocks often fall here.

If you plan to invest in the stock market to meet intermediate-term goals, consider large, established companies or dividend-paying companies in industries that provide the necessities of life (such as the food and beverage industry, pipelines, or electric utilities). In today's economic environment, stocks attached to companies that serve basic human needs should have a major presence in most Canadian stock portfolios. They're especially well-suited for intermediate investment goals and are also well represented in the Canadian stock market.

TIP Just because a particular stock is labelled as being appropriate for the intermediate term doesn't mean you should get rid of it by the stroke of midnight five years from now. After all, if the company is doing well and going strong, you can continue holding the stock indefinitely. The more time you give a well-positioned, profitable company's stock to grow, the better you'll do.

The long term

Stock investing is best suited for making money over a long period of time. Usually, when you measure stocks against other investments in terms of five to (preferably) ten or more years, they excel. Even investors who bought stocks during the depths of the Great Depression saw profitable growth in their stock portfolios over a ten-year period. In fact, if you examine any ten-year period over the past 50 years, you see that stocks beat out other financial investments (such as bonds or bank investments) in most periods when measured by total return (taking into account reinvesting and compounding of capital gains and dividends).

Of course, your work doesn't stop at deciding on a long-term investment. You still have to do your homework and choose stocks wisely, because even in good times, you can lose money if you invest in companies that go out of business. Chapters 5 and 6 show you how to evaluate specific companies and industries and alert you to factors in the general economy and in companies that can affect stock behaviour.

Because so many different types and categories of stocks are available, virtually any Canadian with a long-term perspective should add some stocks to his investment portfolio. Whether you want to save for a young child's university fund or for future retirement goals, carefully selected stocks have proven to be a superior long-term investment.

How to Invest for a Purpose

When someone asked the couple why they bungee jumped off the bridge that spanned a massive ravine, they answered, "Because it's fun!" When someone asked the couple why they dove into a pool chockfull of alligators and snakes, they responded, "Because someone pushed us." You shouldn't invest in stocks unless you have a purpose that you understand, such as investing for growth or income. Keep in mind that stocks are just a means to an end: Figure out your desired end and then match the means. The following sections can help.

TIP: Even if an advisor pushes you to invest, be sure that advisor gives you an explanation of how each stock choice fits your purpose. Here's an example: One nice, elderly couple had a portfolio brimming with aggressive-growth stocks because they had an overbearing broker. Their purpose should've been conservative, and they should've chosen investments that would preserve their wealth rather than grow it. Obviously, the broker's agenda got in the way. (To find out more about dealing with brokers and advisors, go to Chapter 4.)

Growth investing

When investors want their money to grow (versus just trying to preserve it), they look for investments that *appreciate,* or grow, in value. If you bought a stock for $8 per share and now its value is $30 per share, your investment has grown by $22 per share — that's appreciation.

Appreciation (also known as *capital gain*) is probably the number-one reason that people invest in stocks. Few investments have the potential to grow your wealth as conveniently as stocks.

TIP

Stocks are a great way to grow your wealth, but they're not the only way. Many investors seek alternative ways to make money, but many of these alternative ways are more aggressive than stocks and carry significantly more risk. You may have heard about people who made quick fortunes in areas such as commodities (wheat, pork bellies, precious metals, and so on), options, and other more sophisticated and exotic investment vehicles. Keep in mind that you should limit these riskier investments to only a small portion of your portfolio, such as 5 or 10 percent of your investable funds, and you should always understand the type of security (stock, bond, and so on) and the company you're invested in. Experienced investors, however, can go higher.

Income investing

Not all investors want to take on the risk that comes with making a killing. Some people just want to invest in the stock market as a means of providing a steady income and preserving wealth. They don't need stock values to go through the ceiling. Instead, they need stocks that perform well consistently.

If your purpose for investing in stocks is to create income, you need to choose stocks that pay dividends. Dividends are typically paid quarterly to stockholders on record as of specific dates. How do you know if the dividend you're being paid is higher (or lower) than other vehicles (such as bonds)? The following sections help you figure it out.

Dividends versus interest

Don't confuse dividends with interest. Most people are familiar with interest because that's how you grow your money over the years in the bank. The important difference is that interest is paid to creditors, and dividends are paid to owners (meaning shareholders — and if you own stock, you're a shareholder because shares of stock represent ownership in a publicly traded company).

When you buy stock, you buy a piece of that company. When you put money in a bank (or when you buy bonds), you basically loan your money. You become a creditor, and the bank or bond issuer is the debtor; as such, it must eventually pay your money back to you with interest.

The importance of an income stock's yield

When you invest for income, you have to consider your investment's after-tax yield and compare it with the alternatives. The *yield* is an investment's payout expressed as a percentage of the investment amount. Looking at the yield is a way to compare the income you expect to receive from one investment with the expected income from others. Table 2-1 shows some comparative yields.

Investment	Type	Amount	Pay Type	Payout	Yield
Smith Co.	Stock	$50/share	Dividend	$2.50	5.0%
Jones Co.	Stock	$100/share	Dividend	$4.00	4.0%
Acme Bank	Bank GIC	$500	Interest	$25.00	5.0%
Acme Bank	Bank GIC	$2,500	Interest	$131.25	5.25%
Acme Bank	Bank GIC	$5,000	Interest	$287.50	5.75%
Brown Co.	Bond	$5,000	Interest	$300.00	6.0%

Table 2-1: *Comparing the Yields of Various Investments*

TIP

To calculate yield, use the following formula: yield = payout ÷ investment amount.

For the sake of simplicity, the following exercise is based on an annual percentage yield basis, before tax (compounding would increase the yield).

Jones Co. and Smith Co. are typical dividend-paying stocks. Looking at Table 2-1 and presuming that both companies are similar in most respects (including risk) except for their differing dividends, how can you tell whether the $50 stock with a $2.50 annual dividend is better (or worse) than the $100 stock with a $4.00 dividend? The yield tells you.

Even though Jones Co. pays a higher dividend ($4.00), Smith Co. has a higher yield (5 percent). So, if you have to choose between those two as an income investor, choose Smith Co. Of course, if you truly want to maximize your income and play it a bit safer, and if don't need your investment to appreciate a lot, you should probably choose Brown Co.'s bond because it offers a yield of 6 percent.

Dividend-paying stocks can increase in value and to different extents. They may not have the same growth potential as growth stocks, but at the very least, they have a greater potential for capital gain than GICs or bonds.

How to Invest for Your Personal Style

Your investing style isn't a blue-jeans-versus-three-piece-suit debate. It refers to your approach to stock investing. Do you want to be conservative or aggressive? Would you rather be the tortoise or the hare? Your investment personality greatly depends on your purpose and the term over which you're planning to invest (see the previous two sections). The following sections outline the two most general investment styles.

Conservative investing

Conservative investing means you put your money in something proven, tried, and true. You invest your money in safe and secure places, such as banks and government-backed securities. But how does that apply to stocks? If you're a conservative stock investor, you want to place your money in companies that exhibit some of the following qualities:

- **Proven performance:** You want companies that have shown increasing sales and earnings year after year. You don't demand anything spectacular — just a strong and steady performance.
- **Large market size:** You want to invest in large cap companies (short for large capitalization). In other words, they should have a market value exceeding $5–$25 billion. Conservative investors surmise that bigger is safer.
- **Proven market leadership:** Look for companies that are leaders in their industries, with excellent senior management.
- **Perceived staying power:** You want companies with the financial clout and market position to weather uncertain market and economic conditions. What happens in the economy or who gets elected to the House of Commons shouldn't matter.

As a conservative investor, you don't mind if the companies' share prices jump (who would?), but you're more concerned with steady growth and less risk over the long term. (Risk, in stock investing, is introduced in Chapter 3.)

Aggressive investing

Aggressive investors can plan long-term or look over only the intermediate term, but in any case, they want stocks that resemble jack rabbits — those that show the potential to break out of the pack.

If you're an aggressive stock investor, you want to invest your money in companies that exhibit some of the following qualities:

- **Great potential:** Choose companies that have superior goods, services, ideas, or ways of doing business compared to the competition.
- **Capital gains possibility:** Don't even consider dividends. If anything, you dislike dividends. You feel that the money dispensed in dividend form is better reinvested in the company. This, in turn, can spur greater growth.
- **Innovation:** Find companies that have innovative technologies, ideas, or methods that make them stand apart. These companies often find themselves smack in the middle of emerging trends such as the electrification of vehicles or the legalization of cannabis.

Aggressive Canadian investors usually seek out small capitalization stocks, known as small caps, because they can have plenty of potential for growth. A giant redwood may be strong, but it may not grow much more, whereas a new sapling has plenty of growth to look forward to. Why invest in big, stodgy companies when you can invest in smaller enterprises that may become the leaders of tomorrow? Aggressive investors have no problem buying stock in obscure businesses because they hope that such companies will become another Apple, Amazon, or McDonald's.

3

Gathering Information and Understanding Risk

Knowledge and information are two critical success factors in stock investing. (Isn't that true about most things in life?) Canadians who plunge headlong into stocks without sufficient knowledge of the stock market in general, and current information in particular, quickly learn the lesson of the eager diver who didn't find out ahead of time that the pool was only an inch deep (ouch!). In their haste not to miss so-called golden investment opportunities, investors too often end up losing money.

Successful investors are masters at getting the right information — financial and non-financial — and understanding risk.

TIP

For the best approach to stock investing, build your knowledge and find quality information first so you can make your fortune more assuredly. Before you buy, you need to know that the company you're investing in is

- Financially sound and growing (profitable and not excessively indebted)
- Offering products and services that are in demand by consumers
- In a strong and growing industry (and general economy)

Where do you start, and what kind of information do you want to acquire? Keep reading.

Stock Exchanges

Before you invest in stocks, you need to be completely familiar with the basics of stock investing. At its most fundamental, stock investing is about using your money to buy a piece of a company that will give you value in the form of appreciation or income (or both). Fortunately, many resources are available to help you find out about stock investing. Some of the best places are the websites of stock exchanges themselves.

Stock exchanges are organized marketplaces for the buying and selling of stocks (and other securities). The New York Stock Exchange (NYSE), NASDAQ, and the Toronto Stock Exchange (TSX) are the premier North American stock exchanges. (TSX is one of several components of the TMX Group of companies.) They provide a framework for stock buyers and sellers to make their transactions. The Toronto and New York exchanges, like all others, make money not only from a cut of every transaction but also from fees (such as listing fees) charged to companies and brokers that are members of their exchanges.

The TSX is one of the world's larger stock exchanges by market capitalization. It offers a range of businesses from Canada and abroad. The TSX, like the NYSE and NASDAQ, offers a wealth of free (or low-cost) resources and information on its website (`https://tsx.com/`) for all stock investors.

TIP

There are peripheral exchanges to be mindful of as well. Formerly known as the American Stock Exchange, NYSE American is an exchange designed for growing companies. In Canada, other exchanges you may see in some newspaper business sections or online include the following:

- **TSX Venture Exchange:** This is a public venture capital stock market for emerging innovative companies that are not yet big enough to be listed on larger exchanges like the TMX.

- **Canadian Securities Exchange (CSE):** Considered to be an alternative stock exchange for entrepreneurs, it is an option for companies looking to access Canadian capital markets. The CSE lists hundreds of micro-cap equities, government bonds, and other financial instruments. The CSE is operated by CNSX Markets Inc.
- **Montreal Exchange (MX):** The MX is low profile in that it's a derivatives exchange — a place to trade futures contracts and options. The MX is a TMX Group component.
- **NASDAQ Canada:** This is a subsidiary of the NASDAQ Stock Market in the U.S. Its purpose is to ensure that Canadian investors have quick availability to all key information of all NASDAQ securities and that companies have the ability to raise capital more efficiently.
- **NEO:** The NEO Exchange, or NEO, aims to help companies and investors by creating a better trading and listing experience (for example, with free stock quotes and faster listing times). The NEO is based in Canada.

On the U.S. side, the Dow Jones Industrial Average (DJIA) is the most widely watched index worldwide (although technically it's not an index, it's still used as one). It tracks 30 widely owned, large cap stocks, and is occasionally rebalanced to drop (and replace) a stock that's not keeping up. The NASDAQ Composite Index covers a cross-section of stocks from NASDAQ. It's generally considered a mix of stocks of high-growth (riskier) companies with a strong representation of technology stocks. The S&P 500 Index tracks 500 leading, publicly traded companies considered to be widely held.

TIP Go to the NYSE, NASDAQ, and TMX websites (TMX includes the TSX and other website links), to find useful resources such as these:

- Tutorials on how to invest in stocks, common investment strategies, and so on
- Glossaries and free information to help you understand the language, practice, and purpose of stock investing
- A wealth of news, press releases, financial data, and other information about companies listed on the exchange or market, usually accessed through an on-site search engine
- Industry analysis and Canadian and foreign news
- Stock quotes and other market information related to the daily market movements of Canadian and other stocks, including data such as volume, new highs, new lows, and so on
- Free tracking of your stock selections (input a sample portfolio or the stocks you're following to see how well you're doing)

What each exchange or market offers keeps changing and is often updated, so explore them periodically at their respective websites:

- **NASDAQ:** `www.nasdaq.com/`
- **New York Stock Exchange:** `www.nyse.com/`
- **Toronto Stock Exchange:** `www.tsx.com/`

The federal and provincial governments have been planning to create a national securities regulator, like the Securities and Exchange Commission in the U.S. (despite trying and failing to do this in the past). The objective is to create a single Canadian securities watchdog, rather than have a dozen or so separate securities regulators in the provinces and territories. Stay tuned to news providers and the resources mentioned in this chapter for further developments.

The Basics of Accounting and Economics

Stocks represent ownership in companies. Before you buy individual stocks, you want to understand the companies whose stock you're considering and find out about their operations.

It may sound like a daunting task, but you'll digest the point more easily when you realize that companies work very similarly to the way you work. They make decisions on a daily basis just like you.

Think about how you grow and prosper as an individual or family, and you see the same issues with businesses and how they grow and prosper. Low earnings and high debt are examples of financial difficulties that can affect both people and companies. You can better understand companies' finances by taking the time to pick up some information in two basic disciplines: accounting and economics. These two disciplines, discussed in the following sections, play a significant role in understanding the performance of a firm's stock.

Accounting

Accounting. Ugh! But face it: Accounting is the language of business, and believe it or not, you're already familiar with the most important accounting concepts. Just look at the following three essential principles:

- **Assets minus liabilities equals net worth.** In other words, take what you own (your *assets*), subtract what you owe (your *liabilities*), and the rest is yours (your *net worth*). Your own personal finances work the same way as Microsoft's (except yours have fewer zeros at the end).

A company's balance sheet shows you its net worth at a specific point in time (such as December 31). The net worth of a company is the bottom line of its asset and liability picture, and it tells you whether the company is *solvent* (has the ability to pay its debts without going out of business). The net worth of a successful company grows regularly. To see whether your company is successful, compare its net worth with the net worth from the same point a year earlier. A firm that had a $4 million net worth last year and has a $5 million net worth this year is doing well; its net worth has gone up 25 percent ($1 million) in one year.

- **Income minus expenses equals net income.** In other words, take what you make (your income), subtract what you spend (your expenses), and the remainder is your *net income* (or *net profit* or *net earnings* — your gain).

  A company's profitability is the whole point of investing in its stock. As it profits, the business becomes more valuable, and in turn, its stock price becomes more valuable. To discover a firm's net income, look at its income statement. Try to determine whether the company uses its gains wisely, either by reinvesting them for continued growth or by paying down debt.

- **Do a comparative financial analysis.** That's a mouthful, but it's just a fancy way of saying how a company is doing now compared with something else (such as a prior period or a similar company).

- If you know that the company you're looking at had a net income of $50,000 for the year, you may ask, "Is that good or bad?" Obviously, making a net profit is good, but you also need to know whether it's good compared to something else. If the company had a net profit of $40,000 the year before, you know that the company's profitability is improving. But if a similar company had a net profit of $100,000 the year before and in the current year is making $50,000, then you may want to either avoid the company making the lesser profit or see what (if anything) went wrong with the company making less.

Accounting can be this simple. If you understand these three basic points of reference, you're ahead of the curve (in stock investing as well as in your personal finances). For more information on how to use a company's financial statements and reports to pick good stocks, see Chapter 5.

How economics affects stocks

Economics. Double ugh! No, you aren't required to understand "the inelasticity of demand aggregates" (thank heavens!) or "marginal utility" (say what?). But having a working knowledge of basic economics is crucial to your success and proficiency as a stock investor. The stock market and the economy are joined at the hip. The good (or bad) things that happen to one have a direct effect on the other. The following sections give you the lowdown.

The basic concepts

TIP

Alas, many Canadian investors get lost on basic economic concepts (as do some so-called experts that you see on TV). Understanding basic economics will help you filter the financial news to separate relevant information from the irrelevant in order to make better investment decisions. Be aware of these important economic concepts:

- **Supply and demand:** How can anyone possibly think about economics without thinking of the ageless concept of supply and demand? *Supply and demand* can be simply stated as the relationship between what's available (the supply) and what people want and are willing to pay for (the demand). This equation is the main engine of economic activity and is extremely important for your stock investing analysis and decision making process. Do you really want to buy stock in a company that makes elephant-foot umbrella stands if you find out that the company has an oversupply and nobody wants to buy them anyway?

- **Cause and effect:** If you pick up a prominent news report and read, "Companies in the table industry are expecting plummeting sales," do you rush out and invest in companies that sell chairs or manufacture tablecloths? Consider that cause and effect is an exercise in logical thinking, and logic is a major component of sound economic thought.

  When you read Canadian and U.S. business news, play it out in your mind. What good (or bad) can logically be expected given a certain event or situation? If you're looking for an effect ("I want a stock price that keeps increasing"), you also want to understand the cause. Some typical events that can cause a stock's price to rise are positive news reports about a company, a company's industry, or a company's customers, and negative news reports about a company's competitors.

  The news may report that the company is enjoying success with increased sales or a new product. BlackBerry's introduction of new security software services to underserved or new markets such as autonomous cars is a perfect example of how news can move the price of a stock one way or another.

  The media may be highlighting that the industry is poised to do well. Or maybe your company is in industry A, but its customers are in industry B. If you see good news about industry B, that may be good news for your stock.

If the competitors are in trouble — say, due to their deficient customer service and poor overall reputation — their customers may seek alternatives to buy from, including your company.

- **Economic effects from government actions:** Political and governmental actions have economic consequences. As a matter of fact, nothing has a greater effect on investing and economics than government. Government actions usually manifest themselves as taxes, laws, or regulations. They also can take on a more ominous appearance, such as war or the threat of war. Government can willfully (or even accidentally) cause a company to go bankrupt, disrupt an entire industry, or even cause a depression. Government controls the money supply, credit, and all public securities markets.

Insight from past mistakes

Because most investors ignored some basic observations about economics during the Great Recession, they subsequently lost trillions in their stock portfolios during 2008–2009. Even today, the U.S. and Canada are experiencing the greatest expansion of total debt in history, coupled with a record expansion of their respective money supplies. To be sure, part of this government behaviour has fueled the recent bull market. But a question to you is when will this "fun" stop? At the time of this writing, the Federal Reserve and the Bank of Canada signalled a tapering of their support.

Of course, you should always be happy to earn double-digit annual returns with your investments, but such a return can't be sustained and encourages speculation. This artificial stimulation by the Federal Reserve in the United States, and to a lesser degree by the Bank of Canada, resulted and to some extent continues to result in the following:

- More and more people depleted their savings. After all, why settle for 1–3 percent in a Canadian chartered bank when you can get 20 percent in the stock market?
- More and more Canadians bought on credit. If the economy is booming, why not buy now and pay later? Canadian consumer credit recently hit record per capita highs.
- More and more Canadians borrowed against their homes. Why not borrow and get rich now? "I can pay off my debt later" was at the forefront of these folks' minds at the time.
- More and more companies sold more goods as consumers took more vacations and bought SUVs, electronics, and so on. Companies then borrowed to finance expansion, open new stores, and so on.

- More and more Canadians made lower and lower down payments, simply because they could. "Why shouldn't I own a house too?" they asked. The risk profile of Canadian homeowners got so bad that the Canada Mortgage and Housing Corporation imposed a minimum percentage down payment limit before it would write any new mortgages. The risk continues to this day as home prices continue to remain high.
- More and more companies went public and offered stock to take advantage of the increase in money that was flowing to the markets from banks and other financial institutions.

In summary, the economic cycle as it relates to stocks goes something like this: North American spending starts to slow down because consumers and businesses become too indebted. This slowdown in turn causes the sales of goods and services to taper off. Companies are left with too much overhead, capacity, and debt because they expanded too quickly. At this point, businesses get caught in a financial bind. Too much debt and too many expenses in a slowing economy mean one thing: Profits shrink or disappear. To stay in business, companies have to do the logical thing — cut expenses. What's usually the biggest expense for companies? People. Many companies start laying off employees. As a result, consumer spending drops further because more people were either laid off or had second thoughts about their own job security.

Because people had little in the way of savings and too much in the way of debt, they had to sell their stock to pay their bills. Stocks drop. This rinse and repeat trend is one major reason that stocks can fall for an extended period.

TIP The lessons from years past are important ones for investors today:

- Stocks aren't a replacement for savings accounts or guaranteed investment certificates (GICs). Always have some money in the bank.
- Stocks should never occupy 100 percent of your investment funds.
- When anyone (including an expert) tells you that the economy will keep growing indefinitely, be skeptical and read diverse sources of information.
- If stocks do well in your portfolio, consider protecting your stocks (both your original investment and any gains) with stop-loss orders.
- Keep debt and expenses to a minimum.
- If the U.S. and Canadian economy is booming, a decline is sure to follow as the ebb and flow of the economy's business cycle continues.

Stock Tables

The stock tables in major business publications such as *The Wall Street Journal* and *Investor's Business Daily* are loaded with information that can help you become a savvy investor — *if* you know how to interpret them. You need the information in the stock tables for more than selecting promising investment opportunities. You also need to consult the tables after you invest to monitor how your stocks are doing.

The *National Post* (`www.nationalpost.com`) and *The Globe and Mail* (`www.theglobeandmail.com`) produce stock tables for a selection of mostly Canadian equities in their print editions. As well, they let you check just about any stock (U.S. or Canadian) in their online editions.

Looking at the stock tables without knowing what you're looking for or why you're looking is the equivalent of reading *War and Peace* backwards through a kaleidoscope — nothing makes sense. But this section can help you make sense of it all (well, at least the stock tables). Table 3-1 shows a sample stock table. Each item gives you some clues about the current state of affairs for that particular company. The sections that follow describe each column to help you understand what you're looking at.

52-Wk High	52-Wk Low	Name (Symbol)	Div	Vol	Yld	P/E	Day Last	Net Chg
21.50	8.00	SkyHighCorp (SHC)		3,143		76	21.25	+0.25
47.00	31.75	LowDownInc (LDI)	2.35	2,735	5.7	18	41.00	–0.50
25.00	21.00	ValueNowInc (VNI)	1.00	1,894	4.5	12	22.00	+0.10
83.00	33.00	DoinBadly Corp (DBC)		7,601			33.50	–0.75

Table 3-1: *A Sample Stock Table*

TIP

Every newspaper's financial tables are a little different, but they give you basically the same information. Updated daily, these tables aren't the place to start your search for a good stock; they're usually where your search ends. The stock tables are the place to look when you own, or are about to own, a stock or know what you want to buy, or possibly sell, and you're just checking to see the most recent price.

52-week high

The column in Table 3-1 labelled *52-Wk High* gives you the highest price that particular stock has reached in the most recent 52-week period. Knowing this price lets you gauge where the stock is now versus where it has been recently. SkyHighCorp's (SHC) stock has been as high as $21.50, whereas its last (most recent) price is $21.25, the number listed in the *Day Last* column. (Flip to the later section "Day last" for more on understanding this information.) SkyHighCorp's stock is trading very high right now because it's hovering near its overall 52-week high figure.

Now, take a look at DoinBadlyCorp's (DBC) stock price. It seems to have tumbled big time. Its stock price has had a high in the past 52 weeks of $83, but it's currently trading at $33.50. Something just doesn't seem right here. During the past 52 weeks, DBC's stock price has fallen dramatically. If you're thinking about investing in DBC, find out why the stock price has fallen. If the company is strong, it may be a good opportunity to buy stock at a lower price. If the company is having tough times, avoid it. In any case, research the firm and find out why its stock has declined. (Chapter 5 provide the basics of researching companies.)

52-week low

The column labelled *52-Wk Low* gives you the lowest price that particular stock reached in the most recent 52-week period. Again, this information is crucial to your ability to analyze stock over a period of time. Look at DBC in Table 3-1, and you can see that its current trading price of $33.50 in the Day Last column is close to its 52-week low of $33.

Keep in mind that the high and low prices just give you a range of how far that particular stock's price has moved within the past 52 weeks. They can alert you that a stock has problems, or they can tell you that a stock's price has fallen enough to make it a bargain. Simply reading the 52-Wk High and 52-Wk Low columns isn't enough to determine which of those two scenarios is happening. They basically tell you to get more information before you commit your money.

Name and symbol

The *Name (Symbol)* column is the simplest in Table 3-1. It tells you the company name (usually abbreviated) and the stock symbol assigned to the company.

When you have your eye on a Canadian or other stock for potential purchase, get familiar with its symbol. Knowing the symbol makes it easier for you to find your stock in the financial tables, which list stocks in alphabetical order by the company's name (or symbol, depending on the source). Stock symbols are part of the language of stock investing, and you need to use them in all stock communications, from getting a stock quote at your broker's office to buying stock over the internet.

Dividend

The dividend is important to investors seeking income from their stock investments. *Dividends* (shown under the *Div* column in Table 3-1) are basically payments to owners (stockholders). If a company pays a dividend, it's shown in the dividend column. The amount you see is the annual dividend quoted for one share of that stock. If you look at LowDownInc (LDI) in Table 3-1, you can see that you get $2.35 as an annual dividend for each share of stock that you own. Companies usually pay the dividend in quarterly amounts. If you own 100 shares of LDI, the company pays you a quarterly dividend of $58.75 ($235 total per year). A healthy company strives to maintain or upgrade the dividend for stockholders from year to year. (Find out more about additional dividend details later in this chapter.)

Volume

Normally, when you hear the word "volume" on the news, it refers to how much stock is bought and sold for the entire market: "Well, stocks were very active today. Trading volume at the New York Stock Exchange hit 2 billion shares." Volume is certainly important to watch because the stocks that you're investing in are somewhere in that activity. For the *Vol* column in Table 3-1, though, the volume refers to the individual stock.

Volume tells you how many shares of that particular stock were traded that day. If only 100 shares are traded in a day, the trading volume is 100. SHC had 3,143 shares change hands on the trading day represented in Table 3-1. Is that good or bad? Neither, really. Usually the business news media mention volume for a particular stock only when it's unusually large. If a stock normally has volume in the 5,000 to 10,000 range and all of a sudden has a trading volume of 87,000, it's time to sit up and take notice.

TIP

Keep in mind that a low trading volume for one stock may be a high trading volume for another stock. You can't necessarily compare one stock's volume against that of any other company. The large cap stocks such as IBM or Microsoft typically have trading volumes in the millions of shares almost every day, whereas less active, smaller stocks may have average trading volumes in far, far smaller numbers.

The main point to remember is that trading volume that is far in excess of that stock's normal range is a sign that something is going on with that stock. It may be negative or positive, but something newsworthy is happening with that company. If the news is positive, the increased volume is a result of more people buying the stock. If the news is negative, the increased volume is probably a result of more people selling the stock. What events typically cause increased trading volume? Some positive reasons include the following:

- **Good earnings reports:** The company announces good (or better-than-expected) earnings.
- **A new business deal:** The firm announces a favourable business deal, such as a joint venture, or lands a big client.
- **A new product, service, or discovery:** The company's research and development department creates a potentially profitable new product, or the company finds something new and of value, such as oil reserves in a northern territory.
- **Indirect benefits:** The business may benefit from a new development in the economy or from a new law passed by Parliament.

Some negative reasons for an unusually large fluctuation in trading volume for a particular stock include the following:

- **Bad earnings reports:** Profit is the lifeblood of a company. When its profits fall or disappear, you see more volume.
- **Governmental problems:** The stock is being targeted by government action, such as a lawsuit or an Ontario Securities Commission (OSC) probe.

- **Liability issues:** The media report that the company has a defective product or similar problem.
- **Financial problems:** Independent analysts report that the company's financial health or cashflow is deteriorating.

Check out what's happening when you hear about heavier-than-usual volume (especially if you already own the stock).

Yield

In general, yield is a return on the money you invest. However, in the stock tables, *yield* (*Yld* in Table 3-1) is a reference to what percentage that particular dividend is of the stock price. Yield is most important to income investors. It's calculated by dividing the annual dividend by the current stock price. In Table 3-1, you can see that the yield du jour of ValueNowInc (VNI) is 4.5 percent (a dividend of $1 divided by the company's stock price of $22). Note that many companies report no yield; because they have no dividends, their yield is zero.

Keep in mind that the yield reported in the financial pages changes daily as the stock price changes. Yield is always reported as if you're buying the stock that day. If you buy VNI on the day represented in Table 3-1, your yield is 4.5 percent. But what if VNI's stock price rises to $30 the following day? Investors who buy stock at $30 per share obtain a yield of just 3.3 percent (the dividend of $1 divided by the new stock price, $30). Of course, because you bought the stock at $22, you essentially locked in the prior yield of 4.5 percent. Lucky you. Pat yourself on the back.

P/E

The *P/E ratio* is the ratio between the price of the stock and the company's earnings. P/E ratios are widely followed and are important barometers of value in the world of stock investing. The P/E ratio (also called the *earnings multiple* or just *multiple*) is frequently used to determine whether a stock is expensive (a good value). Value investors find P/E ratios to be essential to analyzing a stock as a potential investment.

TIP

As a general rule, the P/E should be 10 to 20 for large cap or income stocks. For growth stocks, a greater P/E is generally preferable. (See Chapter 5 for full details on P/E ratios.)

In the P/E ratios reported in stock tables, *price* refers to the cost of a single share of stock. *Earnings* refers to the company's reported earnings per share as of the most recent four quarters. The P/E ratio is the price divided by the earnings. In Table 3-1, VNI has a reported P/E of 12, which is considered a low P/E. Note how SHC has a relatively high P/E (76). This stock is considered too pricey because you're paying a price equivalent to 76 times earnings. Also note that DBC has no available P/E ratio. Usually this lack of a P/E ratio indicates that the company reported a loss in the most recent four quarters.

Day last

The *Day Last* column tells you how trading ended for a particular stock on the day represented by the table. In Table 3-1, LDI ended the most recent day of trading at $41. Some Canadian newspapers report the high and low for that day in addition to the stock's ending price for the day.

Net change

The information in the *Net Chg* column answers the question, "How did the stock price end today compared with its price at the end of the prior trading day?" Table 3-1 shows that SHC stock ended the trading day up 25 cents (at $21.25). This column tells you that SHC ended the prior day at $21. VNI ended the day at $22 (up 10 cents), so you can tell that the prior trading day it ended at $21.90.

How to Minimize Your Risk

Now, before you go crazy thinking that stock investing carries so much risk that you may as well not get out of bed, take a breath. Minimizing your risk in stock investing is easier than you think. Although wealth-building through the stock market doesn't take place without some amount of risk, you can practice the following tips to maximize your profits and still keep your money secure.

Gain knowledge

Some people spend more time analyzing a restaurant menu to choose a $10 entrée than analyzing where to put their next $5,000. Lack of knowledge constitutes the greatest risk for new investors, so diminishing that risk starts with gaining knowledge. The more familiar you are with the stock market — how it works, factors that affect stock value, and so on — the better you can navigate around its pitfalls and maximize your profits. The same knowledge that enables you to grow your wealth also enables you to minimize your risk. Before you put your money anywhere, you want to know as much as you can.

This book is a great place to start — check out the earlier sections of this chapter for a rundown of the kinds of information you want to know before you buy stocks, as well as the resources that can give you the information you need to invest successfully.

Stay out until you get a little practice

If you don't understand stocks, don't invest! Yes, this book is about stock investing, and some measure of stock investing is a good idea for most people. But that doesn't mean you should be 100 percent invested 100 percent of the time.

If you don't understand a particular stock (or don't understand stocks, period), stay away until you do. Instead, give yourself an imaginary sum of money, such as $100,000, think of some reasons to invest, and just make believe (a practice called *simulated stock investing* or *trading*). Choose a few stocks that you think will increase in value, track them for a while, and see how they perform. Begin to understand how the price of a stock goes up and down, and watch what happens to the stocks you choose when various events take place. As you find out more about stock investing, you get better at choosing individual stocks, without risking — or losing — any money during your learning period.

A good place to do your imaginary investing is at a website such as Investopedia's simulator (`www.investopedia.com/simulator`). You can design a stock portfolio and track its performance with thousands of other investors to see how well you do.

Put your financial house in order

Advice on what to do before you invest could be an entire book all by itself. The bottom line is that you want to make sure that you are, first and foremost, financially secure before you take the plunge into the stock market. If you're not sure about your financial security, look over your situation with a financial planner.

Before you buy your first stock, here are a few things you can do to get your finances in order:

- **Have a cushion of money.** Set aside three to six months' worth of your gross living expenses somewhere safe, such as in a bank account or money market fund, in case you suddenly need cash for an emergency.
- **Reduce your debt.** Overindulging in debt continues to be a serious personal economic problem for many Canadians. Recently, the Bank of Canada raised warning signals about the personal levels of debt held by many individuals in this country.

- **Make sure that your job is as secure as you can make it.** Are you keeping your skills up to date? Is the company you work for strong and growing? Is the industry that you work in strong and growing?
- **Make sure that you have adequate insurance.** You need enough insurance to cover your needs and those of your family in case of illness, death, disability, and so on.

Diversify your investments

Diversification is a risk management strategy for reducing risk by spreading your money across different investments. It's a fancy way of saying, "Don't put all your eggs in one basket." But how do you go about divvying up your money and distributing it among different investments? The easiest way to understand proper diversification may be to look at what you *shouldn't* do:

- **Don't put all your money in one stock.** Sure, if you choose wisely and select a hot stock, you may make a bundle, but the odds are tremendously against you. Unless you're a real expert on a particular company, having small portions of your money in several different stocks is a good idea. As a general rule, the money you tie up in a single stock should be money you can do without.

- **Don't put all your money in one industry or country.** Some people own several stocks but their stocks are all in the same industry. Again, if you're an expert in that particular industry, this approach can work out. But just understand that you're not properly diversified. If a problem hits an entire industry, you may get hurt. Similarly, don't have all of your stock holdings in the stock market of one country.
- **Don't put all your money in one type of investment.** Stocks may be a great investment, but you need to have money elsewhere. Bonds, bank accounts, treasury securities, real estate, and precious metals are perennial alternatives to complement your stock portfolio. Some of these alternatives can be found in mutual funds or exchange-traded funds. An *exchange-traded fund (ETF)* is a fund with a fixed portfolio of stocks or other securities that tracks a particular index but is traded like a stock. See Chapter 7 for more information.

TIP Okay, now that you know what you *shouldn't* do, what *should* you do? Until you become more knowledgeable, follow this advice:

- **Keep only 5 to 10 percent (or less) of your investment money in a single stock.** Because you want adequate diversification, you don't want overexposure to a single stock. Aggressive investors can certainly go for 10 percent or even higher, but conservative investors are better off at 5 percent or less.

- **Invest in various industries and hold several stocks in each industry (four or five stocks, and no more than ten, in each).** Which industries? Choose industries that offer products and services that have shown strong, growing demand. To make this decision, use your common sense. Think about the industries that people need no matter what happens in the general economy, such as food, energy, and other consumer necessities. See Chapter 6 for more information about analyzing sectors and industries.

4

Going for Brokers

When you're ready to dive in and start investing in stocks, you first have to choose a broker. It's kind of like buying a car: You can do all the research in the world and know exactly what kind of car you want, but you still need a venue to conduct the transaction. Similarly, when you want to buy stock, your task is to do all the research you can to select the company you want to invest in. Still, you need a Canadian — yes, it has to be a Canadian — broker to buy the stock, whether over the phone or online. This chapter introduces you to the intricacies of the investor/broker relationship.

The Broker's Role

The broker's primary role is to serve as the vehicle through which you either buy or sell stock. When this chapter talks about brokers, it's referring to companies such as TD Waterhouse, BMO InvestorLine, and many other Canadian organizations that can buy stock on your behalf. Brokers can also be individuals who work for such firms. Although you can buy some stocks directly from the companies that issue them, to purchase most stocks, you still need a broker.

TIP: The distinction between institutional stockbrokers and personal stockbrokers is important:

- **Institutional stockbrokers** make money from institutions and companies through investment banking and securities placement fees (such as initial public offerings and secondary offerings), advisory services, and other broker services.
- **Personal stockbrokers** generally offer the same services to individuals and small businesses.

Although the primary task of brokers is the buying and selling of securities around the world (the word *securities* refers to the world of financial or paper investments, and stocks are only a small part of that world), they can perform other tasks for you, including the following:

- **Providing advisory services:** Investors pay brokers a fee for investment advice. Customers also get access to the firm's research.
- **Offering limited banking services:** Brokers can offer features such as interest-bearing Canadian and U.S. dollar trading accounts, cheque writing, electronic deposits and withdrawals, and credit and debit cards.
- **Brokering other securities:** In addition to stocks, brokers can buy bonds, options, exchange-traded funds (ETFs), mutual funds, and other investments on your behalf.

Personal stockbrokers make their money from individual investors like you through various fees, including the following:

- **Brokerage commissions:** This fee is for buying or selling stocks and other securities.
- **Margin interest charges:** This interest is charged to investors for borrowing against their brokerage account for investment purposes.
- **Service charges:** These charges are for performing administrative tasks and other functions. Brokers charge account opening, maintenance, and other fees

to investors for registered retirement savings plans (RRSPs), registered education savings plans (RESPs), and tax-free savings accounts (TFSAs).

Any smaller broker (some individual brokers are now called financial or investment advisors) that you deal with should be a member in good standing of IIROC — Investment Industry Regulatory Organization of Canada. IIROC is a self-regulatory organization that oversees all member investment dealers. It also watches out for suspicious and questionable trading activity on debt and equity markets in Canada. It sets regulatory and investment industry standards, tries to protect investors' interests, and attempts to strengthen market integrity while maintaining smoothly operating capital markets.

To further protect your money after you deposit it into a brokerage account, that broker should be one of the more than 200 members of the Canadian Investor Protection Fund (CIPF). CIPF doesn't protect you from losses from market fluctuations; it protects your money, within limits, in case the brokerage firm goes out of business or if your losses are due to brokerage fraud. CIPF's coverage limit is $1 million for any combination of cash and securities. If you have both a general and a retirement account, each account qualifies for $1 million coverage.

TIP: To find out whether a broker is registered with these organizations, contact IIROC (`www.iiroc.ca`) and CIPF (`www.cipf.ca`).

Full-Service and Discount Brokers

Stockbrokers fall into two basic categories: full-service and discount. The type you choose depends on what type of investor you are. Here are the differences in a nutshell:

- **Full-service brokers** are suitable for investors who need some guidance, advice, and personal attention.
- **Discount brokers** are better for investors who are sufficiently confident and knowledgeable about stock investing to manage with minimal help (usually through the broker's website).

Full-service brokers

Full-service brokers provide two things: brokerage and advisory services. They try to provide as many services as possible for Canadians who open accounts with them. When you open an account at a brokerage firm, a representative is assigned to your account. This representative is usually called an account executive, a registered rep, or a financial advisor by the brokerage firm. This person usually has a securities licence (is registered with IIROC and at a minimum has passed the Canadian Securities Course or an equivalent).

Examples of full-service brokers are HSBC InvestDirect (`www.investdirecttrading.hsbc.ca`), RBC Dominion Securities (`www.rbcds.com/`), and TD Waterhouse's (`www.td.com`) Personalized Wealth Advice service. All brokers now have full-featured websites to give you information about their services. Get as informed as possible before you open your account.

What they can do for you

Your account executive is responsible for assisting you, answering questions about your account and the securities in your portfolio, and transacting your buy and sell orders. Here are some things full-service brokers can do for you:

- **Offer guidance and advice:** The greatest distinction between full-service brokers and discount brokers is the personal attention you receive from your account rep. You get to be on a first-name basis with a full-service broker, and you disclose much information about your finances and financial goals. The rep is there to make recommendations about stocks and funds that are (you hope) suitable for you.
- **Provide access to research:** Full-service brokers can give you access to their investment research department, which can give you in-depth information and

analysis on a particular company. This information can be valuable, but be aware of the pitfalls.

- **Help you achieve your investment objectives:** A good rep gets to know you and your investment goals and *then* offers advice and answers your questions about how specific investments and strategies can help you accomplish your wealth-building goals.
- **Make investment decisions on your behalf:** Many investors don't want to be bothered when it comes to investment decisions. Full-service brokers can make decisions for your account with your authorization (referred to as a *discretionary* account). This service is fine, but be sure to that brokers explain their choices to you.

What to watch out for

Although full-service brokers, with their seemingly limitless assistance, can make life easy for an investor, you need to remember some important points to avoid problems:

- Brokers and account reps are salespeople. No matter how well they treat you, they're still compensated based on their ability to produce revenue for the brokerage firm. They generate commissions and fees from you on behalf of the company. (In other words, they're paid to sell you things.)

- Whenever your rep makes a suggestion or recommendation, be sure to ask why and request a complete answer that includes the reasoning behind the recommendation. A good advisor is able to clearly explain the reasoning behind every suggestion. If you don't fully understand and agree with the advice, don't take it.

- Working with a full-service broker costs more than working with a discount broker. They always charge extra for the advice. Discount brokers, on the other hand, are paid for simply buying or selling stocks for you and therefore cost less. Also, most full-service brokers expect you to invest at least $5,000 to $10,000 just to open an account, although many require higher minimums.
- Handing over decision-making authority to your rep can be a possible negative because letting others make financial decisions for you is always dicey — especially when they're using *your* money. If they make poor investment choices that lose you money, you may not have any recourse because you authorized them to act on your behalf.
- Some brokers engage in an activity called churning. *Churning* is basically buying and selling stocks for the sole purpose of generating commissions. Churning is great for brokers but really bad for customers. If your account shows a lot of activity, ask for justification.

Commissions, especially by full-service brokers, can take a big bite out of your wealth, so don't tolerate churning or other suspicious activity.

Discount brokers

Perhaps you don't need any hand-holding from a broker (that'd be kinda weird anyway). You know what you want, and you can make your own investment decisions. All you need is a convenient way to transact your buy/sell orders. In that case, go with a discount broker. These brokers let you buy or sell stocks two ways: through the internet or by phone (touch tone, automated voice prompt, or via a live representative). They offer no advice or premium services — just the basics required to perform your stock transactions.

Canadian discount brokers, as the name implies, are cheaper to engage than full-service brokers. Because you're advising yourself (or getting advice and information from third parties such as newsletters, hotlines, or independent advisors), you can save on costs you'd incur if you used a full-service broker.

TIP

If you choose to work with a discount broker, you must know as much as possible about your personal goals and needs. You have a greater responsibility for conducting adequate research to make good stock selections, and you must be prepared to accept the outcome, whatever that may be.

For a while, the regular Canadian investor had two types of discount brokers to choose from: conventional discount brokers and internet discount brokers. But the two are basically synonymous now, so the differences are hardly worth mentioning. Through industry consolidation in Canada, most of the conventional discount brokers today have fully featured websites, while internet discount brokers have adapted by adding more telephone and face-to-face services. There really are no more pure discount brokers left.

What they can do for you

Discount brokers offer some significant advantages over full-service brokers:

- **Lower cost:** This lower cost is usually the result of lower commissions, and it's the primary benefit of using discount brokers.
- **Unbiased service:** Because they don't offer advice, discount brokers have no vested interest in trying to sell you any particular stock.
- **Access to information:** Established discount brokers offer extensive educational materials at their offices or on their websites. In this regard, they can provide you with valuable passive advice.

What to watch out for

Of course, doing business with discount brokers also has its downsides, including the following:

- **No guidance:** Because you've chosen a discount broker, you *know* not to expect guidance, but the broker should make this fact clear to you anyway. If you're a knowledgeable investor, the lack of advice is considered a positive thing — no interference.
- **Hidden fees:** Discount brokers may shout about their lower commissions, but commissions aren't their only way of making money. Many discount brokers charge extra for services that you may think are included, such as issuing a stock certificate or mailing a statement. Ask whether they assess fees for maintaining tax-deferred savings accounts like RRSPs or for transferring stocks and other securities (such as bonds) in or out of your account, and find out what interest rates they charge for borrowing through brokerage accounts.
- **Minimal customer service:** If you deal with an internet brokerage firm, find out about its customer service. If you can't transact business on its website, find out where you can call for assistance with your order.

How to Choose a Broker

Before you choose a broker, you need to analyze your personal investing style (as explained in Chapter 2), and then you can proceed to finding the kind of broker that fits your needs. It's almost like choosing shoes; if you don't know your size, you can't get a proper fit (and you can be in for an uncomfortable future).

TIP When it's time to choose a broker, keep the following points in mind:

- Match your investment style with a brokerage firm that charges the least amount of money for the services you're likely to use most frequently.
- Compare all the costs of buying, selling, and holding stocks and other securities through a broker. Don't compare only commissions; compare other costs, too, such as margin interest and other service charges.
- Use broker comparison services available in financial publications such as *Report on Business* and *Maclean's* (and, of course, their websites) and online sources such as Canoe Money (`https://canoe.com/category/business/moneywise-pro`).

Finding brokers is easy. Just search for *Canadian online discount brokers* in your favorite search engine. The search results will also pull up many online articles rating each broker and itemizing their services and fees.

Canadian Robo-Advisors

More than a dozen robo-advisors operate in Canada today. This number is expected to increase as the popularity of the platform continues to grow. Some of the names, which you may recognize through Canadian TV and radio commercials, are listed in the following list. Almost all of these have been established since 2015, and most but not all operate across Canada:

- BMO SmartFolio
- Idema Investments
- Invisor
- Justwealth
- ModernAdvisor
- Nest Wealth
- Questrade Portfolio IQ
- RoboAdvisors+
- VirtualWealth
- Virtual Brokers Wealth Management
- Wealthsimple

Not just for millennials

You may be thinking that financial technology is the plaything of millennials, and robo-advisors are just for the young. Well, it turns out that both millennials as well as older Canadians are very much at ease within an online investment advice platform. Both age cohorts interact well with robo-advisor interfaces.

Research indicates that the average age of Canadian robo-advisor customers is about 45 years old. In fact, the average age of robo-advisor customers, depending on the robo-advisor, ranges from as low as 34 to as high as 50 years old. In the United States, about half of robo-advisor clients are over 35 years old.

Asset allocation: What is the robo-advisor investing money in?

Chapter 1 stresses the importance of age, risk appetite, personal goals, return objectives, and other factors in stock investment allocation decisions. With robo-advisors, it's no different. (Again, there is no *robot* — just a simple but smart computer managed and supported by a person who will execute your portfolio.)

It starts with *you*. Your robo-advisor journey begins with you telling the robo-advisor (a company) a bit about yourself. Based on that little human-to-robot chat, the robo-advisor will recommend a certain exchange-traded fund (ETF) or array of ET funds that will suit your needs. The number of portfolio choices ranges from five (which appears to be the current norm) up to ten or more funds.

TIP: Most Canadian robo-advisors invest your funds in ETFs. Those that don't invest exclusively in ETFs, such as RoboAdvisors+ and WealthBar, also invest in mutual funds, pooled funds, and private funds. Typical and main ETF providers across all of Canada's robo-advisors include BMO, Vanguard, Horizons, iShares, Purpose, and many more ETF providers.

Each recommended ETF portfolio is usually top-heavy with *stock* equities and bolstered with some non-equities. Stocks within the ETF will come in different flavours. They may be Canadian, U.S., global (outside Canada and the U.S.), or any combination of stocks. ETFs may also include real estate investment trusts and other equity asset categories such as emerging market equities or sectors such as commodities.

Some of the sexier ETFs will delve into concepts such as futures, sectors such as commodities and cannabis, and themes such as growth. The ETFs recommended by your robo-advisor may be capped off with fixed-income (non-equity) components and financial instruments such as high-quality investment-grade bonds, lower-quality but higher-return corporate bonds, and money market funds.

The allocation possibilities are many and go even further than this section indicates. Your portfolios can be embedded within registered retirement savings plans (RRSPs), tax-free savings accounts (TFSAs), and (if you're older) registered retirement income funds (RRIFs).

After that comes another key feature: You can, should you choose, turn over the day-to-day management of your portfolio to the robo-advisor. You can even choose between robo-advisor offerings that come with passive asset allocation approaches (where the ETF portfolio mirrors a market index) or active asset management (which focuses on outperforming the stock benchmark indexes by buying and selling securities and not sitting still).

TIP

Finally, most robo-advisors can execute free or low-fee automatic portfolio rebalances and tax-loss harvesting — which is a big deal because these duties can be time consuming, tedious, and costly under the traditional investment advisor model.

What to watch for

The first thing to watch for with robo-advisors is the very thing that is obvious from the preceding section: Your investment vehicle choice is often skewed towards ETFs. This fact is neither a good or bad thing. It simply restricts your potential for outsized returns, unless of course the ETF your robo-advisor recommends is of a higher growth but higher risk variety (for example, emerging market or high technology stock). Most robo-advisors also offer commission-free trading, and many commission-free trading platforms are starting to introduce robo-advisor services. It's sometimes hard to tell who focuses on what.

The second risk area is that robo-advisors vary in the extent and nature of the "personal touch" advice they provide and the time of day when such advice can be accessed. Some robo-advisors pitch the word *advice* in every second sentence yet offer very little of it. Again, note that the robos are there to give you the solution to an algorithmic equation. They give you options and a recommendation. You still have to make a few decisions after that.

TIP

Finally, even though robo-advisors are regulated more stringently than human advisors, that regulation deals with governance and business processes. What may *not* be governed, and where your exposure lies, is in the fact that the algorithms may be flawed or even hacked and destroyed at your expense. Speaking of hacking, your personal data may even be stolen. There is no such thing as 100 percent data security.

Fees

Fees are low with robo-advisors, and that is a key appeal. Low fees are possible because robo-advisors don't have to incur the type of office space overhead that financial advisors of similar profile require. Robo-advisors save the most, however, by the fact that they automate so much of their key administrative and operational business processes such as registration, monitoring, and reporting to you. The key operational saving stems from the fact that a computer, not a higher-priced human advisor, does the thinking and solving for you. If that human advisor is not even qualified or properly trained — and many are not — you are really getting fleeced.

Every robo-advisor has a distinct fee structure. Some levy a flat rate. Most charge a certain percentage fee. Others utilize a hybrid of flat and percentage fees. Still others charge more (up to 7 percent with Nest Wealth) with lower balances but drastically reduce the fee after you reach higher minimum balances. Some, such as WealthBar and Wealthsimple, charge fees that are well below 1 percent across a wide range of portfolio balances.

In general, though, robo-advisor clients often pay fees under 1 percent even if they have a limited amount to invest. Investors who are just beginning their stock-investing journey can open accounts with minimums of $5,000 — and in other cases a lot less. In many cases, robo-advisors that invest in Canada's less-expensive ETFs can charge about one half of a percentage point. One thing that's certain is that they compete as lower-cost alternatives to traditional advisors.

Make no mistake, though: The quality of advice you can get from traditional fee for service advisors, assuming they are experienced and certified, is going to be deeper and broader in scope. It's just that they typically charge at least 2 percent of your portfolio size in total fees. If you have a very large portfolio, that can build to thousands and tens of thousands of dollars in total annual fees.

TIP Do the fee math before selecting a robo-advisor.

5

Using Accounting Basics to Choose Winning Stocks

Too often, the only number investors look at when they look at a stock is the stock price quote. Yet what really drives the stock price is the company behind that single number. To make a truly good choice in the world of stocks, you have to consider the company's essential financial information. What does it take to see these important numbers?

This book in your hands and a little work on your part are all you need to succeed. This chapter takes the mystery out of the numbers behind the stock. The most tried-and-true method for choosing a good stock starts with choosing a good company. Choosing a company means looking at its products, services, industry, and financial strength. Considering the problems that the market has witnessed in recent years — such as corporate debt problems and derivative meltdowns wreaking havoc on public companies and financial firms around the world — this chapter is more important than ever. Don't underestimate it. Because accounting is the language of business, understanding the basics behind the numbers can save your portfolio.

How to Recognize Value When You See It

If you choose a stock based on the value of the underlying company that issues it, you're a *value investor* — an investor who looks at a company's value to judge whether you can purchase the stock at a good price. Companies have value the same way many things have value, such as eggs or elephant-foot umbrella stands. And there's a fair price to buy them at, too. Take eggs, for example. You can eat them and have a tasty treat while getting nutrition as well. But would you buy an egg for $1,000 (and no, you're not a starving millionaire on a deserted island)? Of course not. But what if you could buy an egg for 10 cents? At that point, it has value and a good price. This kind of deal is a value investor's dream.

Value investors analyze a company's fundamentals (earnings, assets, and so on) to see whether the information justifies purchasing the stock. They see whether the stock price is low relative to these verifiable, quantifiable factors. Therefore, value investors use fundamental analysis, whereas other investors may use technical analysis. Technical analysis looks at stock charts and statistical data, such as trading volume and historical stock prices. Some investors use a combination of both strategies.

History has shown that the most successful long-term investors have typically been value investors using fundamental analysis as their primary investing approach. The most consistently successful long-term investors were — and are — predominately value investors. Here, we describe different kinds of value and explain how to spot a company's value in several places.

Different types of value

Value may seem like a murky or subjective term, but it's the essence of good stockpicking. You can measure value in different ways (as you discover in the following sections), so you need to know the differences and understand the effect that value has on your investment decisions.

Market value

TIP

When you hear someone quoting a stock at $47 per share, that price reflects the stock's market value. The total market valuation of a company's stock is also referred to as its *market cap* or *market capitalization.* How do you determine a company's market cap? With the following simple formula: Market capitalization = share price × number of shares outstanding.

If Canuck Corp.'s stock is $35 per share and it has 10 million shares outstanding (or shares available for purchase), its market cap is $350 million. Granted, $350 million may sound like a lot of money, but Canuck Corp. is considered a small cap stock.

Who sets the market value of stock? The market, of course. Millions of investors buying and selling directly and through intermediaries such as mutual funds determine the market value of any particular stock. If the market perceives that the company is desirable, investor demand for the company's stock pushes up the share price.

The problem with market valuation is that it's not always a good indicator of a good investment. In recent years, plenty of companies have had astronomical market values, yet they've proven to be risky investments. For example, think about Valeant Pharmaceuticals, which for a brief period several years ago was the largest company on the TMX in terms of market capitalization. Shares of Valeant reached $335 at its peak. Then things went south. An acquisition spree that drove its share price up left the company buried in debt. That and a catastrophic combination of controversial drug price hikes and an alleged multimillion-dollar kickback scheme caused those shares to tumble to as low as $12.75. After a few years and a name change later (it's now Bausch Health Companies), the company has since recovered. But the damage to the legacy company's reputation still places pressure on the stock price of Bausch Health Companies today.

Because market value is a direct result of the buying and selling of stock investors, it can be a fleeting thing. This precariousness is why investors must understand the company behind the stock price.

Book value and intrinsic value

Book value (also referred to as *accounting value*) looks at a company from a balance sheet perspective (assets – liabilities = net worth, or stockholders' equity). It's a way of judging a firm by its net worth to see whether the stock's market value is reasonable compared to the company's intrinsic value. *Intrinsic* value is tied to what the market price of a company's assets — both tangible (such as equipment) and intangible (such as patents) — would be if sold.

Generally, market value tends to be higher than book value. If market value is substantially higher, the value investor becomes more reluctant to buy that particular stock — it's overvalued. The closer the stock's market capitalization is to the book value, the safer the investment, if the company is well-run.

TIP

Be cautious with a stock whose market value is more than twice its book value. If the market value is $1 billion or more and the book value is $500 million or less, that's a good indicator that the business may be overvalued, or valued at a higher price than its book value and capability to generate a profit. Just understand that the further the market value is from the company's book value, the more you'll pay for the company's real potential value. And the more you pay, the greater the risk that the company's market value (the stock price, that is) can decrease.

Sales value and earnings value

A company's intrinsic value is directly tied to its capability to make money. For this reason, many analysts like to value stocks from the perspective of the company's income statement. Two common and very important barometers of value are expressed in ratios: the price-to-sales (P/S) ratio and the price-to-earnings (P/E) ratio. In both instances, the price is a reference to the company's market value (as reflected in its share price). Sales and earnings are references to the firm's capability to make money. These two ratios are covered more fully in the later section "Tool around with ratios."

TIP

For investors, the general approach is clear. The closer the market value is to the company's intrinsic value, the better. And, of course, if the market value is lower than the company's intrinsic value, you have a potential bargain worthy of a closer look. Part of looking closer means examining the company's income statement (which is discussed later in this chapter), also called the profit and loss statement, income statement, or simply the P&L. A low price-to-sales ratio is 1 or below (say, for example, 0.7), a medium P/S is between 1 and 2, and a high P/S is 3 or higher.

Put the pieces together

When you look at a company from a value-oriented perspective, here are some of the most important items to consider (see the later section "How to Account for Value" for more information):

- **The balance sheet, to figure out the company's net worth:** A value investor buys a company's stock not because it's cheap but because it's *undervalued* (the company is worth more than the price its stock reflects — its market value is as close as possible to its book value).
- **The income statement, to figure out the company's profitability:** A company may be undervalued from a simple comparison of the book value and the market value, but that doesn't mean it's a screaming buy. For example, what if you find out that a company is in trouble and losing money this year? Do you buy its stock then? No, you don't. Why invest in the stock of a losing company? (If you do, you aren't investing — you're gambling or speculating.) The heart of a firm's value, besides its net worth, is its ability to generate profit and cash.

- **Ratios that let you analyze just how well (or not so well) the company is doing:** Value investors basically look for a bargain. That being the case, they generally don't look at companies that everyone is talking about, because by that point the stock of those companies ceases to be a bargain. The value investor searches for a stock that will eventually be discovered by the market and then watches as the stock price goes up. But before you bother digging into the fundamentals to find that bargain stock, first make sure that the company is making money.

The more ways that you can look at a company and see value, the better:

- **Examine the P/E ratio.** One of the first things to look at is the P/E ratio. Does the company have one? (This question may sound dumb, but if the company is losing money, it may not have one.) Does the P/E ratio look reasonable, or is it in triple-digit, nosebleed territory?
- **Check out the debt load.** Next, look at the company's *debt load* (the total amount of liabilities). Is it less than the company's equity? Are sales healthy and increasing from the prior year? Does the firm compare favourably in these categories versus other companies in the same industry? This piece of information is critical because high debt loads can quickly destroy a company in today's unforgiving economy.

- **Think in terms of tens.** There's beauty in simplicity. You'll notice that the number ten comes up frequently in measuring a company's performance, juxtaposing all the numbers you need to be aware of. If net income is rising by 10 percent or more, that's fine. If the company is in the top 10 percent of its industry, that's great. If the industry is growing by 10 percent or better (sales and so on), that's terrific. If sales are up 10 percent or more this year, that's wonderful. A great company doesn't have to have all these things going for it, but it should have as many of these things happening as possible to ensure greater potential success.

Does every company or industry have to neatly fit these criteria? No, of course not. But it doesn't hurt you to be as picky as possible. You need to find only a handful of stocks from thousands of choices.

Value investors can find thousands of companies that have value, but they can probably buy only a handful at a truly good price. The number of stocks that can be bought at a good price is relative to the market. In mature *bull markets* (ones in a prolonged period of rising prices), a good price is hard to find; most stocks have probably seen significant price increases, but in *bear markets* (markets in a prolonged period of falling prices), good companies at bargain prices are easier to come by and represent great stock investing opportunities.

How to Account for Value

Profit is to a company what oxygen is to a human. Without profit, a company can't survive, much less thrive. Without profit, it can't provide jobs, pay taxes, or invest in new products, equipment, or innovation. Without profit, it eventually goes bankrupt, and the price of its stock plummets toward zero.

In the heady days leading up to both of the last two bear markets, many investors lost a lot of money simply because they invested in stocks of companies that weren't making a profit. Lots of public companies ended up like bugs that just didn't see the windshield coming their way. Companies such as Nortel and Lehman Brothers entered the graveyard of rather-be-forgotten stocks. Stock investors as a group lost trillions of dollars investing in glitzy or derivative-fuelled companies that sounded good but weren't making money. When their brokers were saying, "buy, buy, buy," their hard-earned money was saying, "bye, bye, bye!" What were they thinking?

Stock investors need to pick up some rudimentary knowledge of accounting to round out their stock-picking prowess and to be sure that they're getting a good value for their investment dollars. As mentioned, accounting is the language of business. If you don't understand basic accounting, you'll have difficulty being a successful investor. Investing without accounting knowledge is like travelling without a map. However, if you can run a household budget, using accounting analysis to evaluate stocks is easier than you think, as you find out in the following sections.

TIP: Finding the relevant financial data on a company isn't difficult in the age of information and 24-hour internet access. Websites such as `www.nasdaq.com` and `www.sedar.com` can give you the most recent balance sheets and income statements of most public companies.

Break down the balance sheet

TIP: A company's balance sheet gives you a financial snapshot of what the company looks like in terms of the following equation: Assets – liabilities = net worth (or net equity).

The following sections list questions that a balance sheet can answer and explain how to use it judge a company's strength over time.

A few balance sheet questions

Analyze the following items that you find on the balance sheet:

- **Total assets:** Have they increased from the prior year? If not, was it because of the sale of an asset or a write-off (uncollectable accounts receivable, for example)?
- **Financial assets:** In recent years, many companies (especially U.S. banks and some Canadian resource companies) had questionable financial assets (such as subprime mortgages and heavy debt loads) that went bad, and they had to write them off as unrecoverable losses or sell large assets to meet debt repayment obligations. Does the company you're analyzing have a large exposure to financial assets that are low-quality (and hence, risky) debt?
- **Inventory:** Is inventory higher or lower than last year? If sales are flat but inventory is growing, that may be a problem, perhaps caused by obsolete inventory.
- **Debt:** Debt may be the biggest weakness on the corporate balance sheet. Make sure that debt isn't a growing item and that it's under control. In recent years, debt has become a huge problem.
- **Derivatives:** A *derivative* is a speculative and complex financial instrument that doesn't constitute ownership of an asset (such as a stock, bond, or commodity) but is a promise to convey ownership. Some derivatives

are acceptable because they're used as protective or hedging vehicles (this use isn't a primary concern). But they're frequently used to generate income and can then carry risks that can increase liabilities. Standard options and futures are examples of derivatives on a regulated exchange, but the derivatives this section is talking about are a different animal and in an unregulated part of the financial world. Some economists estimate that the worldwide derivatives market is more than ten times the total world gross domestic product. The number or value often mentioned is one *quadrillion,* or 1,000 times one trillion dollars. These stratospheric numbers can easily devastate a company, sector, or market (as the credit crisis and Great Recession of over a decade ago showed).

TIP

Find out whether the company dabbles in these complicated, dicey, leveraged financial instruments. Find out (from the company's regulatory filings in SEDAR or EDGAR) whether it has derivatives and, if so, the total amount. Having derivatives that are valued higher than the company's net equity may cause tremendous problems. Derivatives problems sank many, ranging from stodgy banks (Barings Bank of England) to affluent counties (Orange County, California) to once-respected hedge funds (LTCM) to corporations (Lehman Brothers).

- **Equity:** *Equity* is the company's net worth (what's left in the event that all the assets are used to pay off all the company debts). The stockholders' equity should be increasing steadily by at least 10 percent per year. If not, find out why.

Table 5-1 shows you a brief example of a balance sheet.

Assets (What the Company Owns)	Amount
1. Cash and inventory	$5,000
2. Equipment and other assets	$7,000
3. TOTAL ASSETS (Item 1 + Item 2)	$12,000
Liabilities (What the Company Owes)	
4. Short-term debt	$1,500
5. Other debt	$2,500
6. TOTAL LIABILITIES (Item 4 + Item 5)	$4,000
7. NET EQUITY (Item 3 – Item 6)	$8,000

Table 5-1: *XYZ Balance Sheet — December 31, 2019*

By looking at a company's balance sheet, you can address the following questions:

- **What does the company own (assets)?** The company can own assets, which can be financial, tangible, and intangible. An asset is anything that has value or that can be converted to or sold for cash.

  Financial assets can be cash, investments (such as stocks or bonds of other companies), or accounts receivable.

Tangible assets can be items such as inventory, equipment, or buildings. Intangible things can be licences, patents, trademarks, copyrights, and so on. For example, companies such as Facebook and Alphabet (which is better known as Google and includes its other subsidiaries) are not just enormous cash asset generators — they also have tremendously valuable patent, licence, and other intangible or intellectual property assets.

- **What does the company owe (liabilities)?** A *liability* is anything of value that the company must ultimately pay someone else for. Liabilities can be invoices (accounts payable) or short-term or long-term debt.
  - Watch liabilities carefully when you study financial statements. If they are growing quickly when other parts of the business, such as sales, are not doing well or keeping pace, this may spell trouble.
- **What is the company's net equity (net worth)?** After you subtract the liabilities from the assets, the remainder is called *net worth, net equity,* or *net stockholders' equity.* This number is critical when calculating a company's book value.

A company's financial strength over time

The logic behind the assets/liabilities relationship of a company is the same as that of your own household. When you look at a snapshot of your own finances (your personal balance sheet), how can you tell whether you're doing well? Odds are that you start by comparing some numbers. If your net worth is $5,000, you may say, "That's great!" But a more appropriate remark is something like, "That's great compared to, say, a year ago."

TIP

Compare a company's balance sheet at a recent point in time to a past time. You should do this comparative analysis with all the key items on the balance sheet, which are listed in the preceding section, to see the company's progress (or lack thereof). Is it growing its assets or shrinking its debt or both? Most important, is the company's net worth growing? Has it grown by at least 10 percent since a year ago? All too often, Canadian investors stop doing their homework after they make an initial investment. You should continue to look at the firm's numbers regularly so that you can be ahead of the curve. If the business starts having problems, you can get out before the rest of the market starts getting out (which causes the stock price to fall).

TIP

To judge the financial strength of a company, ask the following questions:

- **Are the company's assets greater in value than they were three months ago, a year ago, or two years ago?**

Compare today's asset size (especially tangible asset size) to the most recent two years to make sure that the company is growing in size and financial strength.

- **How do the individual items compare with prior periods?** Some particular assets that you want to take note of are cash, inventory, and accounts receivable.
- **Are liabilities such as accounts payable and debt about the same, lower, or higher compared to prior periods? Are they growing at a similar, faster, or slower rate than the company's assets?** Debt that rises faster and higher than items on the other side of the balance sheet is a key warning sign of potential financial problems.
- **Is the company's net worth or equity greater than the preceding year? And is that year's equity greater than the year before?** In a healthy company, the net worth is constantly rising. As a general rule, in good economic times, net worth should be at least 10 percent higher than the preceding year. In tough economic times (such as a recession), 5 percent is acceptable. Seeing the net worth grow at a rate of 15 percent or higher is great. Don't lose sight of this very important financial indicator.

TIP

When evaluating a stock, look under the management discussion and analysis (MD&A) section of the annual report for discussion about commitments, contingencies, and pledged assets. Determine roughly how big the potential effect can be if some of these commitments turn into reality.

Whenever the economy goes into a period of recession, many Canadian and U.S. companies will suffer losses. This typically qualifies them for tax credits to be received in a future tax period. Many companies will recognize this as a special item (revenue) on the income statement in the current year to boost the bottom line. A tax asset is also booked on the balance sheet. Invariably, after a year or so, window dressers make the tax asset (tax credit receivable) disappear — the company reevaluates the likelihood of qualifying for the credit and determines that it stands no chance of collecting from the CRA or Uncle Sam. The tax asset gets written off, a special charge is created (in the year a company would prefer to see a charge), and the investor is left with even more distorted financial statements.

Many, if not most, public companies have pension plans for employees, and corresponding obligations to adequately fund those plans. If there's any deficiency in the amount that's contributed to the plan, the company ultimately has to fund the shortfall. Cash infusions dig into the company's cash balances and can potentially impair its capability to do the things it wants to. During any challenging economic period, this becomes an important issue. Many companies will fail to adjust downward the assumptions underpinning their pension plans, such as the returns the plan's investments will generate in upcoming years. Some pension plans are still based on assumptions that their investment funds will grow at 7 percent or more, when in fact future forecasted returns are expected to be lower.

Look at the income statement

Where do you look if you want to find out what a company's profit is? Check out the firm's *income statement*. It reports, in detail, a simple accounting equation that you probably already know: Sales – expenses = net profit (or net earnings, or net income).

Look at the following figures found on the income statement:

- **Sales:** Are they increasing? If not, why not? By what percentage are sales increasing? Preferably, they should be 10 percent higher than the year before. Sales are, after all, where the money comes from to pay for all the company's activities (such as expenses) and create subsequent profits.

- **Expenses:** Do you see any unusual items? Are total expenses reported higher than the prior year, and if so, by how much? If the total is significantly higher, why? A company with large, rising expenses will see profits suffer, which isn't good for the stock price.
- **Research and development (R&D):** How much is the company spending on R&D? Companies that rely on new product development (such as pharmaceuticals or biotech firms) should spend at least as much as they did the year before (preferably more) because new products mean future earnings and growth.
- **Earnings:** This figure reflects the bottom line. Are total earnings higher than the year before? How about earnings from operations (leaving out expenses such as taxes and interest)? The earnings section is the heart and soul of the income statement and of the company itself. Out of all the numbers in the financial statements, earnings have the greatest single impact on the company's stock price.

Table 5-2 shows you a brief example of an income statement.

Looking at the income statement, investors can try to answer these questions:

- **What sales did the company make?** Businesses sell products and services that generate revenue (known as sales or gross sales). Sales also are referred to as the *top line*.

Total Sales (Or Revenue)	Amount
1. Sales of products	$11,000
2. Sales of services	$3,000
3. TOTAL SALES (Item 1 + Item 2)	$14,000
Expenses	
4. Marketing and promotion	$2,000
5. Payroll costs	$9,000
6. Other costs	$1,500
7. TOTAL EXPENSES (Item 4 + Item 5 + Item 6)	$12,500
8. NET INCOME (Item 3 – Item 7) (In this case, it's a net profit)	$1,500

Table 5-2: *XYZ Income Statement for Year Ending 12/31/2019*

- **What expenses did the company incur?** In generating sales, companies pay expenses, such as payroll, utilities, advertising, and administration.
- **What is the net profit?** Also called *net earnings* or *net income, net profit* is the bottom line. After paying for all expenses, what profit did the company make?

The information you glean should give you a strong idea about a firm's current financial strength and whether it's successfully increasing sales, holding down expenses, and ultimately maintaining profitability. You can find out more about sales, expenses, and profits in the sections that follow.

Sales

Sales refers to the money that a company receives as customers buy its goods or services. It's a simple item on the income statement and a useful number to look at. Analyzing a business by looking at its sales is called top line analysis.

TIP Investors should take into consideration the following points about sales:

- **Sales should be increasing.** A healthy, growing company has growing sales. They should grow at least 10 percent from the prior year, and you should look at the most recent three years. The extent to which sales increase from quarter to quarter greatly influences a stock's price movement, one way or another.
- **Core sales (sales of those goods or services that the company specializes in) should be increasing.** Frequently, the sales figure has a lot of stuff lumped into it. Maybe the company sells widgets (what the heck is a widget, anyway?), but the core sales shouldn't include other things, such as the sale of a building or other one-time or unusual items. Take a close look. Isolate the firm's primary and regular offerings and ask whether these sales are growing at a reasonable rate (such as 10 percent).

- **Does the company have odd items or odd ways of calculating sales?** Many companies boost their sales by aggressively offering affordable financing with easy repayment terms. Say you find out that Suspicious Sales Inc. (SSI) had annual sales of $50 million, reflecting a 25 percent increase from the year before. Looks great. But what if you find out that $20 million of that sales number comes from sales made on credit that the company extended to non-creditworthy buyers? Some companies that use this approach later have to write off losses as uncollectable debt because the customers ultimately can't pay for the goods.

TIP

If you want to get a good clue as to whether a company is artificially boosting sales, check its accounts receivable (listed in the asset section of its balance sheet). Accounts receivable refers to money that is owed to the company for goods that customers have purchased on credit. If you find out that sales went up by $10 million (great) but accounts receivable went up by $20 million (uh-oh), something just isn't right. That may be a sign that the financing terms were too easy, and the company may have a problem collecting payment (especially in a recession).

Expenses

How much a company spends has a direct relationship to its profitability. If spending isn't controlled or held at a sustainable level, it may spell trouble for the business.

TIP When you look at a company's expense items, consider the following:

- **Compare expense items to the prior period.** Are expenses higher than, lower than, or about the same as those from the prior period? If the difference is significant, you should see commensurate benefits elsewhere. In other words, if overall expenses are 10 percent higher compared to the prior period, are sales at least 10 percent more during the same period? If advertising expenses are up, did sales rise in a meaningful and predictable way?
- **Are some expenses too high?** Look at the individual expense items. Are they significantly higher than the year before and as compared to industry peers? If so, why?
- **Have any unusual items been expensed?** An unusual expense isn't necessarily a negative. Expenses may be higher than usual if a company writes off uncollectable accounts receivable as a bad debt expense. Doing so inflates the total expenses and subsequently results in

lower earnings. Pay attention to nonrecurring charges that show up on the income statement, and determine whether they make sense.

Profit

Earnings, or *profit*, is the single most important item on the income statement. It's also the one that receives the most attention in the financial media. When a company makes a profit, it's usually reported as earnings per share (EPS). So if you hear that XYZ Corporation beat last quarter's earnings by a penny, here's how to translate that news. Suppose that the company made $1 per share this quarter and 99 cents per share last quarter. If that company had 100 million shares of stock outstanding, its profit this quarter is $100 million (the EPS times the number of shares outstanding), which is $1 million more than it made in the prior quarter ($1 million is 1 cent per share times 100 million shares).

TIP

Don't simply look at current earnings as an isolated figure. Always compare current earnings to earnings in past periods (usually a year). For example, if you're looking at a retailer's fourth-quarter results, don't compare them with the retailer's third-quarter outcome. Doing so is like comparing apples to oranges. What if the company usually does well during the December holidays but poorly in the fall? In that case, you don't get a fair comparison.

A strong company should show consistent earnings growth from the period before (the prior year or the same quarter from the prior year), and you should check the period before that, too, so that you can determine whether earnings are consistently rising over time. Earnings growth is an important barometer of the company's potential growth and bodes well for the stock price.

TIP

When you look at earnings, here are some things to consider:

- **Total earnings:** This item is the most watched. Total earnings should grow year to year by about 10 percent and more.
- **Operational earnings:** Break down the total earnings and look at a key subset — that portion of earnings derived from the company's core and regular activity. Is the company continuing to make money from its primary goods and services?
- **Nonrecurring items:** Are earnings higher (or lower) than usual or than expected, and if so, why? Frequently, the difference results from irregularly occurring and atypical items such as the sale of an asset or a large depreciation write-off.

You can keep percentages as simple as possible. A good number is 10 percent because it's easy to calculate and it's a good benchmark. However, 5 percent isn't unacceptable if you're talking about tough times, such as a recession. Obviously, if sales, earnings, and/or net worth are hitting or surpassing 15 percent, that's great.

Some retailers, and especially internet e-tailers, use coupon promotions to promote higher sales volumes. That's fine. What is not fine is when companies engage in window dressing where they exclude the value (cost) of promotional giveaways when booking revenue. They have found a more dubious approach. Assume for a moment that someone buys a gadget for $30 and uses a $10 coupon to make the purchase. Under generally accepted accounting rules, just $20 of revenue ought to be booked. But some retailers would book $30 in revenue and charge the $10 in promotional costs to marketing expenses. The auditors should catch this, but sometimes they don't. Such accounting high jinks may result in artificially higher sales and gross margin, better top-line comments from financial analysts, and inflated share price. Can you spell "distortion"?

A company can turn a variety of what should be expenses into assets by depreciating capital assets (resources that last more than one year) more slowly than otherwise required under the principle of reasonableness (in other words, by easing it slowly into expenses). With certain types of costs incurred, management can judgmentally overestimate a period of useful benefit to longer than one year. That would let management justify recording part of it on the balance sheet (as an asset) instead of on the income statement (as an expense). This serves to artificially boost profits.

Tool around with ratios

A *ratio* is a helpful numerical tool that you can use to find out the relationship between two or more figures found in a company's financial data. A ratio can add meaning to a number or put it in perspective. Ratios sound complicated, but they're easier to understand than you may think.

Say that you're considering a stock investment and the company you're looking at has earnings of $1 million this year. You may think that's a nice profit, but for this amount to be meaningful, you have to compare it to something. What if you find out that the other companies in the industry (of similar size and scope) had earnings of $500 million? Does that change your thinking? Or what if the same company had earnings of $75 million in the prior period? Does that change your mind?

Two key ratios to be aware of are

- Price-to-earnings (P/E) ratio
- Price-to-sales (P/S) ratio

Every investor wants to find stocks that have a 20 percent average growth rate over the past five years and have a low P/E ratio (sounds like a dream). Use stock screening tools available for free on the internet to do your research. A stock screening tool lets you plug in numbers, such as sales or earnings, and ratios, such as the P/E ratio or the debt to equity ratio, and then click — up come stocks that fit your criteria. These tools are a good starting point for serious investors. Most Canadian brokers have them at their websites, such as TD Waterhouse (www.tdwaterhouse.ca or www.td.com/ca/en/investing) and BMO InvestorLine (www.bmo.com/investorline). Some excellent stock screening tools and filters can also be found at TMX (www.tmxmoney.com), Bloomberg (www.bloomberg.com), NASDAQ (www.nasdaq.com), and MarketWatch (www.marketwatch.com).

The P/E ratio

The *price-to-earnings (P/E) ratio* is important in analyzing a potential stock investment because it's one of the most widely regarded barometers of a company's value, and it's usually reported along with the company's stock price in the financial page listing. The major significance of the P/E ratio is that it establishes a direct relationship between the bottom line of a company's operations — the earnings (or net profit) — and the stock price.

The *P* in P/E stands for the stock's current price. The *E* is for earnings per share (typically the most recent 12 months of earnings). The P/E ratio is also referred to as the *earnings multiple* or just *multiple.*

TIP: You calculate the P/E ratio by dividing the price of the stock by the earnings per share. If the price of a single share of stock is $10 and the earnings (on a per-share basis) are $1, then the P/E is 10. If the stock price goes to $35 per share and the earnings are unchanged, then the P/E is 35. Basically, the higher the P/E, the more you pay for the company's earnings.

Why would you buy stock in one company with a relatively high P/E ratio instead of investing in another company with a lower P/E ratio? Investors buy stocks based on expectations. They may bid up the price of the stock (subsequently raising the stock's P/E ratio) because they feel that the company will have increased earnings in the near future. Perhaps they feel that the company has great potential (a pending new invention or lucrative business deal) that will eventually make it more profitable. More profitability in turn has a beneficial effect on the firm's stock price. The danger with a high P/E is that if the company doesn't achieve the hoped-for results, the stock price can fall.

Look at two P/E ratios to get a balanced picture of the company's value:

- **Trailing P/E:** This P/E is the most frequently quoted because it deals with existing data. The trailing P/E uses the most recent 12 months of earnings in its calculation.
- **Forward P/E:** This P/E is based on projections or expectations of earnings in the coming 12-month period. Although this P/E may seem preferable because it looks into the near future, it's still considered an estimate that may or may not prove to be accurate.

The following example illustrates the importance of the P/E ratio. Say that you want to buy a business and someone you know is selling a business. You go to that person and say, "What do you have to offer?" The person says, "Have I got a deal for you! I operate a retail business downtown that sells spatulas. The business nets a cool $2,000 profit per year." You say, "Uh, okay, what's the asking price for the business?" The reply? "You can have it for only $1 million!" What do you say?"

If you're sane, odds are that you politely turn down that offer. Even though the business is profitable (a cool $2,000 a year), you'd be crazy to pay a million bucks for it. In other words, the business is way overvalued (too expensive for what you're getting in return for your investment dollars). The million dollars would generate a better rate of return elsewhere and probably with less risk. As for the business, the P/E ratio of 500 ($1 million divided by $2,000) is outrageous — definitely an overvalued company, and a lousy investment.

What if the person offered the business for $12,000? Does that price make more sense? Yes. The P/E ratio is a more reasonable 6 ($12,000 divided by $2,000). In other words, the business pays for itself in about 6 years (versus 500 years in the prior example).

TIP Looking at the P/E ratio offers a shortcut for investors asking the question, "Is this stock overvalued?" As a general rule, the lower the P/E, the safer (or more conservative) the stock is. The reverse is more noteworthy: The higher the P/E, the greater the risk.

When someone refers to a P/E as high or low, you have to ask the question, "Compared to what?" A P/E of 30 is considered very high for a large cap electric utility but quite reasonable for a small cap, high-technology firm. Keep in mind that phrases such as *large cap* and *small cap* are just a reference to the company's market value or size. *Cap* is short for *capitalization* (the total number of shares of stock outstanding × the share price).

TIP The following basic points can help you evaluate P/E ratios:

- **Compare a company's P/E ratio with its industry.** Electric utility industry stocks, for example, generally have a P/E that hovers in the 9–14 range. So, an electric utility with a P/E of 45 indicates something is wrong with that utility. (Turn to Chapter 6 for more on analyzing industries.)
- **Compare a company's P/E with the general market.** If you're looking at a small cap stock on the NASDAQ that has a P/E of 100 but the average P/E for established companies on the NASDAQ is 40, find out why. You should also compare the stock's P/E ratio with the P/E ratio for major indexes such as the Dow Jones Industrial Average (DJIA), the Standard & Poor's 500 (S&P 500), the S&P/TSX Composite, and the NASDAQ Composite. Stock indexes are useful for getting the big picture (see Chapter 3).
- **Compare a company's current P/E with recent periods** (such as this year versus last year). If it currently has a P/E ratio of 20 and it previously had a P/E ratio of 30, you know that either the stock price has declined or earnings have risen. In this case, the stock is less likely to fall. That bodes well for the stock.
- **Low P/E ratios aren't necessarily a sign of a bargain,** but if you're looking at a stock for many other reasons that seem positive (solid sales, strong industry, and so on) and it also has a low P/E, that's a good sign.

- **High P/E ratios aren't necessarily bad,** but they do mean that you should investigate further. If a company is weak and the industry is shaky, heed the high P/E as a warning sign. Often, a high P/E ratio means that investors have bid up a stock price, anticipating future income. This situation is common in the fast-growing technology sector.
- **Watch out for a stock that doesn't have a P/E ratio.** In other words, it may have a price (the P), but it doesn't have earnings (the E). No earnings means no P/E, meaning that you're better off avoiding the stock. Can you still make money buying a stock with no earnings? You can, but you aren't investing; you're speculating.

The P/S ratio

The *price-to-sales (P/S) ratio* is a company's stock price divided by its sales. Because the sales number is rarely expressed as a per-share figure, it's easier to divide a company's total market value (explained earlier in this chapter) by its total sales for the last 12 months.

TIP

As a general rule, a stock trading at a P/S ratio of 1 or less is a reasonably priced stock worthy of your attention. For example, say that a company has sales of $1 billion and the stock has a total market value of

$950 million. In that case, the P/S is 0.95. In other words, you can buy $1 of the company's sales for only 95 cents. All things being equal, that stock may be a bargain.

Analysts use the P/S ratio as an evaluation tool in these circumstances:

- In tandem with other ratios to get a more well-rounded picture of the company and the stock.
- When they want an alternative way to value a business that doesn't have earnings.
- When they want a true picture of the company's financial health because sales are tougher for companies to manipulate than earnings.
- When they're considering a company offering products (versus services). The P/S ratio is more suitable for companies that sell items that are easily counted (such as products). Firms that make their money through loans, such as banks, aren't usually valued with a P/S ratio because deriving a usable P/S ratio for them is more difficult.

TIP Compare the company's P/S ratio with other companies in the same industry, with the industry average, to get a better idea of the company's relative value.

6

Sectors, Small Caps, and the Cannabis Space

Suppose you have to bet your entire nest egg on a one-kilometre race. All you need to do is select a winning group. Your choices are the following:

- Group A: Thoroughbred race horses
- Group B: Overweight Elvis impersonators
- Group C: Lethargic snails

This isn't a trick question, and you have one minute to answer. Note that you weren't asked to pick a single winner out of a giant mush of horses, Elvii, and snails; you were asked only to pick the winning group in the race. The obvious answer is the thoroughbred race horses (and no, they weren't ridden by the overweight Elvis impersonators, because that would take away from the eloquent point being made). In this example, even the slowest member of Group A easily outdistances the fastest member of either Group B or C.

Industries, like groups A, B, and C in the example, aren't equal, and life isn't fair. After all, if life were fair, Elvis would be alive and the impersonators wouldn't exist. Fortunately, picking stocks doesn't have to be as difficult as picking a winning racehorse. The basic point is that it's easier to pick a successful stock from a group of winners (a growing, vibrant industry). Understanding industries only enhances your stock-picking strategy.

Successful, long-term investor look at the industry (or the basic sector) just as carefully as they look at the individual stock. Luckily, choosing a winning industry to invest in is easier than choosing individual stocks, as you find out in this chapter. Some investors can pick a winning stock in a losing industry, and some investors have chosen a losing stock in a winning industry (the former is far outnumbered by the latter). Just think how well you can do when you choose a great stock in a great industry. Of course, if you repeatedly choose bad stocks in bad industries, you may as well get out of the stock market altogether (maybe your calling is to be a celebrity impersonator instead).

The Difference between a Sector and an Industry

Very often, investors confuse an industry with a sector. Even though it may not be a consequential confusion, some clarity is needed here.

TIP

A *sector* is simply a group of interrelated industries. An *industry* is typically a category of business that performs a more precise activity; you can call an industry a subsector. Investing in a sector and investing in an industry can mean different things for the investor. The result of your investment performance can also be different.

Healthcare is a good example of a sector that has different industries, such as pharmaceuticals, drug retailers, health insurance, hospitals, and medical equipment manufacturers. And within the individual healthcare industries are public companies such as Shoppers Drug Mart, Sun Life Financial, and others that trade on Canadian and other stock exchanges.

TIP

Healthcare is a great example of why you should know the distinction between a sector and an industry. Within a given sector (such as healthcare), you have industries that behave differently during the same economic conditions. Some of the industries are cyclical (such as medical equipment manufacturers), whereas some are defensive (such as drug retailers). In a bad economy, cyclicals tend to go down while defensive stocks generally hold their value. In a good or booming economy, cyclicals do very well while defensive stocks tend to lag. (Find out more about cyclical and defensive industries later in this chapter.)

Given that fact, an exchange-traded fund (ETF) that reflects the general healthcare sector would be generally flat because some of the industries that went up would be offset by those that went down. Flip to Chapter 7 for more about ETFs.

Questions to Ask about Sectors and Industries

Your common sense is an important tool in choosing sectors and industries with winning stocks. This section explores some of the most important questions to ask yourself when you're choosing a sector or industry.

Which category is the industry fall in?

Most industries can be placed neatly in one of two categories: cyclical and defensive. In a rough way, these categories generally translate into what society wants and what it needs. Society buys what it wants when times are good and holds off when times are bad. It buys what it needs in both good and bad times. A want is a "like to have," whereas a need is a "must have."

Cyclical industries

TIP

Cyclical industries are industries whose fortunes rise and fall with the Canadian economy's rise and fall. In other words, if the economy and the stock market are doing well, Canadian consumers and investors are confident and tend to spend and invest more money than usual, so cyclical industries tend to do well. Real estate and automobiles are great examples of cyclical industries.

Your own situation offers you some common-sense insight into the concept of cyclical industries. Think about your behaviour as a consumer, and you get a revealing clue into the thinking of millions of consumers. When you (and millions of others) feel good about your career, your finances, and your future, you have a greater tendency to buy more (or more expensive) stuff. When people feel financially strong, they're more apt to buy a new house or car, or make some other large financial commitment. Also, Canadians take on more debt because they feel confident that they can pay it back. In light of this behaviour, what industries do you think would do well?

The same point holds for business spending. When businesses think that economic times are good and foresee continuing good times, they tend to spend more money on large purchases such as new equipment or technology. They think that when they're doing well and are flush with financial success, reinvesting that money in the business to increase future success is a good idea.

Defensive industries

Defensive industries are industries that produce goods and services that are needed no matter what's happening in the economy. Your common sense kicks in here, too. What do you buy even when times are tough? Think about what millions of Canadians buy no matter how bad the economy gets. A good example is food — people still need to eat regardless of good or bad times. Other examples of defensive industries are utilities and healthcare.

TIP

In bad economic times, and during periods of rising inflation, defensive stocks tend to do better than cyclical stocks. However, when times are good, cyclical stocks tend to do better than defensive stocks.

Defensive stocks don't do as well in good times because Canadians don't necessarily eat twice as much or use up more electricity.

How do defensive stocks grow? Their growth generally relies on two factors:

- **Population growth:** As more and more Canadian consumers are born, more people become available to buy things.
- **New markets:** A company can grow by seeking out new groups of consumers to buy its products and services. Coca-Cola and Maple Leaf Foods, for example, were both early movers that found brand new markets in Asia. As pure communist regimes fell from power and more societies embraced a free market and consumer goods, the companies sold more beverages and food items, and their stocks rose a lot.

TIP

One way to invest in a particular industry is to take advantage of exchange-traded funds (ETFs), which have become popular in recent years. ETFs are structured much like mutual funds but are fixed portfolios that trade like a stock. If you find a winning industry but you can't find a winning stock (or don't want to bother with the necessary research), ETFs are a great consideration. You can find out more about ETFs at websites such as `www.etfdb.com` or by turning to Chapter 7.

Is the sector growing?

Ask yourself whether the sector is growing. The answer may seem obvious, but you still need to ask it before you purchase stock. The saying "the trend is your friend" applies when choosing a sector in which to invest, as long as the trend is an upward one. If you look at three different stocks that are equal in every significant way but you find that one stock is in a sector growing 15 percent per year while the other two stocks are in sectors that have either little growth or are shrinking, which stock would you choose?

Sometimes the stock of a financially unsound or poorly run company goes up dramatically because the sector it's in is exciting to the public. The most obvious example is internet stocks from two decades ago. Stocks such as Nortel shot up to incredible heights because investors thought the internet was the place to be. Sooner or later, however, the measure of a successful company is its capability to be profitable. Serious investors look at the company's fundamentals (refer to Chapter 5 to find out how to do this) and the prospects for the industry's growth before settling on a particular stock.

TIP: Various information sources monitor all the sectors and industries and measure their progress and trends. Some reliable and well-known sources include the following:

- Canoe Money (`https://canoe.com/category/business/`)
- *The Globe and Mail* (`www.theglobeandmail.com`)
- MarketWatch (`www.marketwatch.com`)
- *National Post* (`www.nationalpost.com`)
- Standard & Poor's (`www.spglobal.com/ratings/en`)
- *The Wall Street Journal* (`www.wsj.com`)
- Yahoo! Finance (`https://finance.yahoo.com`)
- Yahoo! Finance Canada (`https://ca.finance.yahoo.com`)

The preceding sources generally give you in-depth information about the major sectors and industries. Visit their websites to read their current research and articles along with links to relevant sites for more details. For example, *The Globe and Mail* and *The Wall Street Journal* both publish current indexes for all the major sectors (such as commodities) and industries (such as oil and gas, copper, corn, and gold) so that you can get a useful snapshot of how well each one is doing.

Standard and Poor's (S&P) Industry Survey is an excellent source of information on U.S. and Canadian industries. Besides ranking and comparing industries and informing you about their current prospects, the survey also lists the top companies by size, sales, earnings, and other key information. Each industry is covered in a few pages, so you get the critical information you need without reading a novel. The survey and other S&P publications are available on the S&P website or in the business reference section of most large libraries. (Your best bet is to head for the library because the survey is expensive.)

Are the sector's products or services in demand?

Look at the products and services that are provided by a sector or an industry. Do they look like things that society will continue to want? Are there products and services on the horizon that could replace them? What does the foreseeable future look like for the sector?

When evaluating future demand, look for a *sunrise industry* — one that's new or emerging or has promising appeal for the future. Good examples of sunrise industries in recent years are cannabis, electric vehicles, biotech, and internet social media, which includes companies such as Groupon, Facebook, and Canada's Shopify and Lightspeed Commerce. In contrast, a *sunset industry* is one that's either declining or has little potential for growth. For example, you probably shouldn't invest in the DVD manufacturing industry because demand has already shifted towards digital content delivery. Owning stock in a strong, profitable company in a sunrise industry is obviously the most desirable choice.

Current research unveils the following megatrends:

- **The aging of Canada:** More senior citizens than ever are living in North America. Because of this fact, financial and healthcare services that touch on eldercare or the financial concerns of the elderly will prosper.
- **Advances in high technology:** Internet, fintech, artificial intelligence, blockchain, telecom, social media, autonomous and electric cars, medical, and biotechnology innovations will continue.
- **Security concerns:** Terrorism, international tensions, and security issues on a personal level mean more attention for national defence, homeland security, cyber security, and related matters.
- **Health care matters:** New vaccine technology and innovation, cannabis for pharmaceutical as well as

recreational use, biotechnology, and wearable devices continue to enjoy a lot of attention and innovation today and should do so into the future.

- **Energy challenges:** Traditional and nontraditional sources of energy (such as solar, battery technology, and electrification of vehicles) will demand society's attention as it faces shrinking supplies of the world's available crude oil.

What does the industry's growth rely on?

An industry doesn't exist in a vacuum. External factors weigh heavily on its capability to survive and thrive. Does the industry rely on an established megatrend? Then it will probably be strong for a while. Does it rely on factors that are losing relevance? Then it may begin to decline soon. Technological and demographic changes are other factors that may contribute to an industry's growth or fall.

TIP

Keep in mind that a sector will continue to grow, shrink, or be level, but individual industries can grow, shrink, or even be on a track to disappear. If a sector is expanding, you may see new industries emerge. For example, the greying of the U.S. and Canada is an established megatrend. As millions of North Americans climb into their later years, profitable opportunities await companies that are prepared to cater to them. Perhaps an industry (subsector) offers great new medical products for senior citizens. Maybe autonomous electric car manufacturers such as Tesla may allow senior citizens to safely stay in their cars a lot longer. You can already see these types of trends emerging as Shoppers Home Health Care stores and Tesla dealerships open across Canada. What are the prospects for continued growth?

Is the industry dependent on another industry?

Industries frequently are intertwined and can become codependent. When one industry suffers, you may find it helpful to understand which industries will subsequently suffer. The reverse can also be true — when one industry is doing well, other industries may reap the benefits.

In either case, if the stock you choose is in an industry that's highly dependent on other industries, you should know about it. If you're considering stocks of resort companies and you see the headlines blaring, "Airlines losing money as public stops flying," what do you do? This type of question forces you to think logically and consider cause and effect. Logic and common sense are powerful tools that frequently trump all the number-crunching activity performed by analysts.

Who are the leading companies in the industry?

After you've chosen the industry, what types of companies do you want to invest in? You can choose from two basic types:

- **Established leaders:** These companies are considered industry leaders or have a large share of the market. Investing in these companies is the safer way to go, as long as their debt loads (if any) to sustain market share and growth are reasonable. What better choice for novice investors than companies that have already proven themselves?
- **Innovators:** If the industry is hot and you want to be more aggressive in your approach, investigate companies that offer new products, patents, or technologies. These companies are probably smaller but have a greater potential for growth in a proven industry.

Is the industry a target of government action?

You need to know if Parliament is targeting an industry, because intervention by politicians and bureaucrats (rightly or wrongly) can have an effect on an industry's economic situation. Find out about any political issues that face a company, industry, or sector.

Investors need to take heed when political "noise" starts coming out about a particular industry. An industry can be hurt either by direct government intervention or by the threat of it. Intervention can take the form of lawsuits, investigations, taxes, regulations, or sometimes an outright ban. In any case, being on the wrong end of government intervention is one of the greatest external threats to a company's survival.

Sometimes, government action helps an industry. Generally, beneficial action takes two forms:

- **Deregulation or tax decreases:** Government sometimes reduces burdens on an industry. A great example is the gradual removal of certain barriers in the medical and recreational marijuana industry in Canada. (Find out more about this sector later in this chapter.) Another example is progressive government deregulation that led the way to more innovation in the telecommunications industry. This trend, in turn, laid the groundwork for more innovation and growth in the internet and the expansion and improvement of cellphone services.
- **Direct funding:** Government has the power to steer taxpayer money toward business as well. In recent years, federal and provincial governments have provided tax

credits and other incentives for alternative energy such as solar power, as well as for an array of individual companies that are leaders in innovation. For example, some time ago, the Government of Canada rolled out an intellectual property (IP) strategy, through which the government intends to increase IP funding and foster an ecosystem that supports business growth, innovation, and competition. Certain public companies listed on the Toronto Stock Exchange will definitely benefit as well.

Traditional and Key Canadian Sectors and Industries

This section highlights some sectors and industries that Canadian stock investors should take note of. Consider investing some of your stock portfolio in those that look promising (and, of course, avoid those that look problematic).

Many investors can benefit from a practice referred to as *sector rotation* (not quite like crop rotation, but close enough). The idea is that you shift money from one sector to another based on current or expectant economic conditions. A number of variations of this concept exist, but in most cases, they follow some essential ideas. If the economy is doing poorly or if the outlook appears bearish, you shift to defensive sectors such as consumer staples and utilities. If the economy is doing well, you shift money to cyclicals such as technology and base materials, which is something that Canada is especially rich in. Given today's fickle economic conditions, sector rotation makes sense and is worth a look by long-term investors. Find out more using the resources mentioned in the section "Is the sector growing?" earlier in this chapter.

Resources and commodities

The Canadian economy is highly concentrated in commodities, as well as other sectors such as bank and consumer goods and services, especially those offerings driven by the real estate sector. The Toronto Stock Exchange (TSX) reflects this unique and integrated ecosystem. Canadian stocks trading on the TSX and other Canadian exchanges are decidedly concentrated in commodities companies such as Barrick, a world-leading gold-mining company, and Suncor Energy, which produces oil. In fact, commodities make up well over 25 percent of the TSX Index. Add to this the fact that the majority of Canadians' portfolios are held in domestic stocks, almost 60 percent, and you can see that this special sector is very important to Canadians.

Note: At the time of this writing, many commodities, such as oil and copper, have been resurging. While the low-hanging fruit may have already been picked off the "value stock" vine, some might still remain. Finding them requires research. However, the purpose of this section is not to identify specific names of winning stocks. Rather, the objective as always is to show you how to pick the winners by focusing on what drives the prices of commodity and other stocks.

What exactly is a commodity?

A *commodity* for stock-investing purposes is a financial instrument, asset, or resource that trades in the *primary* economic sector rather than in the manufactured and value-added products sector. In other words, it's pretty well the stuff you get or grow right from the ground up. Here come the subsets:

- *Soft* commodities are a category of commodities that includes agricultural products such as coffee, wheat, canola, corn, fruit, and sugar.
- *Hard* commodities are also physical resources that are mined, such as gold, copper, diamonds, silver, and oil. That wasn't hard, was it? Drilling these down even further, hard commodities are often subcategorized as *base* metals and *precious* metals.

What drives commodity prices?

Non-commodity asset classes can be driven by the psychology of greed, hype, or fear. Commodities are purer in this regard. At their root, commodities are driven by strong fundamental trends — namely those of supply and demand. These two fundamentals almost always prevail over the longer term, so commodity price movements are somewhat predictable to those who are patient.

World growth remains the main driver of commodity prices. In other words, people will always want and need energy, food, and stuff to build and trade with to be able to move around and just survive.

Moving toward more specific macro drivers, did you know that on an overall basis, Canadian commodity prices are still more heavily influenced by China than by the United States? That's because China is physical goods driven and the U.S. is now more services driven. However, that trading relationship may soon change as Canadian resource companies become more cautious about transacting with China. Nevertheless, commodities continue to fulfill the more physical economic needs of other countries. Another interesting fact that cannot be ignored is that the Canadian stock market, in the context of its global trade nature and heavy commodity profile, remains very highly correlated to the Chinese economy. The moral of this story is that successful Canadian commodity stock investors also keep an eye on the Chinese economy.

Oil, gas, and mining

It has been a rough few years for both oil exploration and development companies and miners. Only now have those that survived the commodities bear market begun to emerge with cleaner balance sheets and good business plans. With recent high oil prices, some oil producers are boosting dividends and buying back shares to support a strong share price. The mining industry, for example, is slowly emerging from the doldrums as well. Stories of growth and discovery of new oil and base metal reserves are now more frequently found in Canadian business news stories. Indicators of the beginning of a recovery in overall commodity production and prices include a resurgence in the number of recent mergers or takeovers. Also, prices for precious metals such as gold and silver are stable if not growing, always a good signal.

TIP

Gold ETFs are based on "electronic gold" that doesn't involve the ownership of physical bullion or the picking of individual stocks. These financial instruments, discussed in Chapter 7, allow Canadians to be exposed to the gold market without the risk of price volatility due to a bad stock pick or pure speculation.

When it comes to oil prices, keep an eye on the essential drivers of demand. In the case of oil, the first elementary driver is demand itself. (Okay, that was easy.) Other drivers of demand and price include OPEC supply and non-OPEC supply decisions you often hear about in the news. Production cuts obviously mean oil will rise in price. Weather, war, and conflict (such as the Ukraine crisis) also drive up oil prices as fears increase that supplies will be curtailed through damage or sanctions. Raw and meaningless speculation in the financial markets also drives oil prices up or down. Finally, national and international strategic petroleum reserves and inventories are reported regularly, so watch out for that news as well.

TIP

Don't just pick one driver in isolation but rather try to paint a bigger picture trend and invest accordingly. After you have first diagnosed the big picture using these criteria, proceed to analyze individual stocks in the manner taught throughout this book.

The last of the big three Canadian commodity sectors mentioned after mining and oil is gold. Gold has multiple drivers you need to watch for as well. The U.S. dollar and U.S. monetary policy go hand in hand, and the strength of the U.S. dollar needs to be watched when investing in gold. The stronger the dollar, typically the weaker the gold price. International demand for jewelry, especially in countries such as India and China, need to be watched as well. At the simple and basic level, gold generates demand from its inherent quality as a store of value. When fiat paper currencies are weak, gold is a strong alternative store of value. Also note that although gold only has about 10 percent use within industrial applications, it is still significant as a driver of price. Finally, other drivers of demand to consider include speculative investment demand, geopolitics, and gold mining activity. Remember: In an inflationary environment, gold prices and the stocks of gold miners often thrive.

Real estate

It's worldwide news that Canada's housing market, especially in Vancouver and Toronto, has reached stratospheric levels. The real estate market actually fueled a significant part (about 1 to 1.5 percent) of the gross domestic product growth of Canada over the last few years. This means that lots of companies associated with real estate — everything from the banks to Home Depot — benefitted from the boom. But how long will this sector growth continue? Will it stabilize or fall? Which companies are affected most by real estate?

The answer to that question depends on your investment time frame. It also depends whether you're referring to residential or commercial real estate, two sub-sectors that are different animals and have different drivers of demand.

Some analysts believe that Canada's hot residential real estate market is getting a big lift from house-hungry millennials and migration into Canada. They expect these two population cohorts to bolster other markets such as Montreal and Ottawa as they consider more affordable options beyond Toronto and Vancouver. Yet all this frothy behaviour may end in the longer term, again because supply tends to catch up to or exceed demand over the long term.

The reason this section highlights Canada's lofty real estate market is because it's a classic example of a cyclical bellwether industry — one that has a great effect on many other industries that may be dependent on it. However, no one imagined it would be this cyclical or powerful. Nevertheless, real estate is always looked at as a key component of economic health because as already mentioned, so many other industries — including building materials, mortgages, household appliances, and contract labour services — are tied to it. A booming real estate industry bodes well for much of the Canadian economy.

TIP: Housing starts are one way to measure real estate activity. This data is an important leading indicator of health in the industry. Housing starts indicate new construction, which means more business for related industries.

TIP: Keep an eye on both the Canadian and U.S. real estate industry for negative news that may be bearish for the domestic economy and the stock market. Because real estate is purchased with mortgage money, investors and analysts watch the mortgage market for trouble signs such as rising delinquencies and foreclosures. These statistics are a warning for general economic weakness.

Discover how to recognize a bubble. In a *bubble,* or *mania,* the prices of the assets such as real estate experience a bull market and skyrocket to extreme levels, which excites more and more investors to jump in, causing prices to rise even further. It gets to the point where seemingly everyone thinks it's easy to get rich by buying this particular asset, and almost no one notices that the market has become unsustainable. After prices are exhausted and start to level off, investor excitement dies down, and then investors try to exit by selling their holdings to realize some profit. As more and more sell off their holdings, demand decreases while supply increases. The mania dissipates, and the bear market appears. If this happens to residential real estate, many stocks of companies that rely on this real estate sub-sector will also enter a bear market.

Financials

Banking and financial services are intrinsic parts of any economy, and Canada's economy is no different. Debt is the most important sign of this industry for investors. If a company's debt is growing faster than the economy, you need to watch how that debt affects stocks. If debt gets out of control, it can be disastrous for the economy.

The amount of debt and debt-related securities recently reached historic and troublesome levels. This was enabled by the still-low interest-rate environment, which makes corporate borrowing cheap and easy. This trend means that many financial stocks of companies like banks that are owed money are at risk if a recession hits anytime soon.

Investors in U.S. and some Canadian financial stocks should be selective in this industry and should embrace only those lenders that are conservative in their balance sheet and are generally avoiding overexposure in areas such as international finance and derivatives.

Small Caps and Speculative Stocks in Any Sector

This chapter is about seizing stock investing opportunities, and most opportunities start on the ground floor. A good example is the cannabis sector, which is discussed later in this chapter. The cannabis sector is speculative, so first you should be armed with some additional and more specific information about new and small capitalization companies before you get into actual cannabis stock-investing principles.

Many of the previously discussed commodity stocks on the S&P/TSX and other Canadian exchanges are also smaller in size and new to the stock market. The very nature of that sector is speculative. Will resource companies find something in the ground or not? That's the daily question they face. Other resource stocks are giants that are established and face a bit less uncertainty.

TIP The key point to keep in mind is that the stocks of emerging companies generally start out as micro or small cap stocks. This chapter is a good place to explore what small cap stock investing is all about if you're considering these stocks.

The attractive potential of small cap stocks

Everyone wants to get in early on a hot new stock. Why not? You buy Shlobotky, Inc., at $1 per share and hope it zooms to $98 before lunchtime. Who doesn't want to buy a cheap stock today that could become the next Apple or Walmart? This possibility is why investors are attracted to small cap stocks.

Small cap (or *small capitalization*) refers to the company's market size. Small cap stocks have a market value between $300 million and $2 billion, arbitrary figures that largely depend on the exchange where they are traded. Investors may face more risk with small caps, but they also have a chance for greater gains. Canada's stock market is replete with small cap stocks.

Out of all the types of stocks, small cap stocks continue to exhibit the greatest amount of growth, but also the greatest volatility. In the same way that a tree planted last year has more opportunity for growth than a mature 100-year-old redwood, small caps have greater growth potential than established large cap stocks. Of course, a small cap doesn't exhibit spectacular growth just because it's small. It grows when it does the right things, such as increasing sales and earnings by producing goods and services that customers want.

TIP

For every small company that becomes a Financial Post FP500 firm, hundreds of companies don't grow at all or go out of business. When you try to guess the next great stock before any evidence of growth, you're not investing — you're speculating. Have you heard that one before? Of course you have, and you'll hear it again. Of course, there's nothing wrong with speculating. But it's important to know when you're speculating. If you're going to speculate in small stocks hoping for the next Alphabet (which includes Google), use the info in the following sections to increase your chances of success.

When to avoid IPOs

Initial public offerings (IPOs) are the birthplaces of public stocks, or the proverbial ground floor. The IPO is the first offering to the public of a company's stock. The IPO is also referred to as "going public." Because a company going public is frequently an unproven enterprise, investing in an IPO can be risky. Here are the two types of IPOs:

- **Start-up IPO:** This is a company that didn't exist before the IPO. In other words, the entrepreneurs get together and create a business plan. To get the financing they need for the company, they decide to go public immediately by approaching an investment banker. If the investment banker thinks it's a good concept, the banker will seek funding (selling the stock to investors) via the IPO.
- **A private company that decides to go public:** In many cases, the IPO is done for a company that already exists and is seeking expansion capital. The company may have been around for a long time as a smaller private concern, but now decides to seek funding through an IPO to grow even larger (or to fund a new product, promotional expenses, and so on). Facebook, Shopify, and Groupon are examples of such IPOs.

Which of the two IPOs do you think is less risky? That's right — the private company going public. Why? Because it's already a proven business, which is a safer bet than a brand-new start-up.

Great stocks started as small companies going public. You may be able to recount the stories of Federal Express, Dell, Home Depot, Shopify, and hundreds of other great successes. But do you remember an IPO by the company Lipschitz & Farquar? No? That's because it's among the majority of IPOs that don't succeed.

TIP

IPOs have a dubious track record of success in their first year. Studies periodically done by the brokerage industry have revealed that IPOs decline in price 60 percent of the time (more often than not) during the first 12 months. In other words, an IPO has a better-than-even chance of dropping in price. For Canadian stock investors, the lesson is clear: Wait until a track record appears before you invest in a company this way. If you don't, you're simply rolling the dice (in other words, you're speculating, not investing). Don't worry about missing that great opportunity; if it's a bona fide opportunity, you'll still do well after the IPO.

Make sure a small cap stock is making money

TIP

Follow these two points when investing in stocks:

- **Make sure a company is established.** Being in business for at least three years is a good minimum.
- **Make sure a company is profitable.** It should show net profits of 10 percent or more over two years or longer.

These points are especially important for investors in small stocks. Plenty of start-up ventures lose money but hope to make a fortune down the road. A good example is a company in the biotechnology industry. Biotech is an exciting area, but it's esoteric, and at this early stage companies are finding it difficult to use the technology in profitable ways. You may say, "But shouldn't I jump in now in anticipation of future profits?" You may get lucky, but you're speculating when you invest in unproven, small cap stocks.

Analyze small cap stocks before you invest

The only difference between a small cap stock and a large cap stock is a few zeros in their numbers and the fact that you need to do more research with small caps. By sheer dint of size, small caps are riskier than large caps, so you offset the risk by accruing more information on yourself and the stock in question. Plenty of information is available on large cap stocks because they're widely followed. Small cap stocks don't get as much press, and fewer analysts issue reports on them.

TIP Here are a few points to keep in mind:

- **Understand your investment style.** Small cap stocks may have more potential rewards, but they also carry more risk. No investors should devote a large portion of their capital to small cap stocks. If you're considering retirement money, you're better off investing in large cap stocks, exchange-traded funds (ETFs; refer to Chapter 7), investment-grade bonds, mutual funds, or a combination thereof. For example, retirement money should be in investments that are either very safe or have proven track records of steady growth over an extended period of time (five years or longer).
- **Check with the SEC and SEDAR.** Get the financial reports that the company must file with the U.S. Securities and Exchange Commission (SEC) and the System for Electronic Document Analysis and Retrieval (SEDAR), such as the company's quarterly reports.
- **Check other sources.** See whether brokers and independent research services, such as Value Line, follow the stock. If two or more different sources like the stock, it's worth further investigation.

Cannabis Stock Investing in Canada

Canada's leadership in the cannabis sector has made the world stand up and take notice. The news about issues surrounding this sector is endless. Where there is change there is also opportunity, and Canadian stock investors are stepping up to the plate to consider adding cannabis stocks in their portfolios.

Whether you use marijuana or simply invest in this budding (no pun intended) industry, you can get into real financial trouble if you don't invest wisely, despite the significant opportunity that this fascinating industry represents. To avoid investment losses in the cannabis space, a good starting point is knowing the unique legal and other challenges the cannabis industry faces (specific risks are covered later in this chapter) — and, of course, reading this book to learn about stock investing and fundamental risk principles.

TIP

Regulations in Canada and the U.S. differ at the municipal, provincial, state, and federal levels. Although cannabis is gaining tremendous momentum in the U.S., the legislative frameworks between the countries are different. Recreational cannabis is federally legal in Canada but not in the U.S. (although it is legal in a growing number of states).

A plant by any other name

In addition to knowing the risk and regulations faced by the business behind any stock, successful stock investors also have to possess a sound grasp and knowledge of the business. (Warren Buffett never invests in businesses he doesn't understand.) A good place to start is to know and understand the special language of the cannabis industry.

Main street lingo: Cannabis 2.0

You can't have a discussion of marijuana or cannabis without the slang. It just wouldn't be cool. Let's begin by knowing that the shredded flowers, buds, and leaves of a marijuana plant come in a green, brown, or grey mix. It's all smelly, but that's in the nose of the beholder.

Marijuana that is rolled up like a cigarette is called a *joint*, and if you roll it like a cigar it's a *blunt*. Marijuana can also be smoked in a pipe. That's just called a *pipe*. Some Canadians incorporate it into cookies or common food, or brew it as a flavoured tea. Canadians who smoke oils from the marijuana plant practice what is referred to as *dabbing*. Other slang names for marijuana include *pot, weed, grass, herb,* or *boom*. It's good to know the lingo, whether you're visit a dispensary to buy weed or investing in cannabis companies. You need to know what these companies make!

It's also interesting to note that smoking weed isn't the dominant industry trend it once was. Quite a few pot users are turning away from the smoking variety of marijuana. The smoke has a problem: People's lungs get coated and choked with tar under long-term use. More and more users are tending toward new ways to consume pot. This is where Cannabis 2.0, as it is referred to, comes in. Cannabis 2.0 represents alternative and often discrete ways to consume, include vapourizing, ingesting oils in capsules or added to food or drink, and applying tinctures directly under the tongue. Cannabis 2.0 also includes various types of beverages, cookies, candies, gummies, and other food items infused with cannabis.

Note: This is not a stock-investing note, but do know that cannabis can make you feel relaxed, silly, sleepy, and happy. It can also make you nervous and scared. Your senses of hearing, sight, and touch may be altered. Your judgment may also be significantly impaired. Okay, back to stock investing.

Bay Street lingo: Cannabis 3.0

The next wave, or Cannabis 3.0, has introduced products that place the benefits of cannabis derivatives squarely in mainstream health products already present in your home, such as pain relief products as well as hand and face creams. You may have seen CBD-infused topical creams and CBD-infused bath bombs in mainstream non-dispensary stores because CBD is not as prohibited as THC in its distribution for recreational use. Cannabis 3.0 includes many more products, such as THC-infused lip balm and THC- or CBD-infused honey.

Innovations with cannabis derivatives will continue — the combinations and possibilities appear endless. Over time, cannabis will become an essential ingredient that you can expect to find in mainstream pharmaceuticals, pet care products, personal hygiene items, and many other product categories. As with alcohol or even snack foods, brands will emerge and become household names in the cannabis sphere. Licensed producers, using industry data to make them stand out from the competitive crowd, will do especially well. Investors in the cannabis space need to keep this product and brand differentiation in mind. It's that important.

Why invest in cannabis stocks?

As with any new industry, good opportunities exist for investors in Canadian cannabis stocks who are willing to do their research. Canada has provided other countries with a legal and operational template for politicians and producers to mimic, and this first-mover advantage in a politically friendly context makes the opportunity to invest in this industry undeniable. The risks associated with any emerging industry — especially cannabis — are many but manageable if you invest carefully.

More than half the states in the U.S. have fully legalized recreational pot. Almost 40 states permit medicinal cannabis, and that number should continue to grow. Pot is already entrenched in the healthcare industry, so it has a small but important base market. What better endorsement is there than a hospital or doctor sanctioning its careful use? As all this slow but steady acceptance is happening, the investment community has swooped in for a piece of the action.

TIP

Companies involved in the cultivation, production, and distribution of weed have many opportunities to access a Canadian stock listing. In Canada, cannabis company listings can be found on the Toronto Stock Exchange (TSX), TSX Venture, and Canadian Securities Exchange (CSE). These and other exchanges are discussed in Chapter 3.

What the past and the present are saying

You can take a look at where Canada has been so far by using numbers, which tell part of a story. According to a recent report from ATB Capital Markets, Canada's recreational marijuana sales could reach almost $5 billion Canadian dollars in 2022, about 20 percent greater than the prior year's estimated figure. For the recreational cannabis market, the report cites a compound annual growth rate (CAGR) of about 14 percent as of 2022, and predicts that cannabis sales could reach over $12 billion by 2030. In contrast, Statista.com estimates that Canada's entire beer brewing industry sales (craft and traditional big brew combined) are estimated to increase to around $10 billion dollars by 2024. Although this apples-and-oranges analysis excludes the additional benefits that the beer industry provides to the hospitality part of our economy, you can see that the raw size of the cannabis market is formidable.

In the U.S., despite the current federal prohibition, research firm BDSA projects legal cannabis sales to reach $30 billion USD in 2022 and about $48 billion USD by 2026, surpassing the American craft beer industry! For additional perspective, the *global* craft beer market is projected to grow from $105 billion in 2022 to $210 billion in 2028. That $30 billion figure is a big enchilada of a number.

Hundreds of Canadian and U.S. publicly listed companies support this ecosystem. You can find most of the big ones at `www.newcannabisventures.com`, a U.S.-oriented site but one that has comprehensive industry analysis and content. For Canadian perspectives, check out `www.bnnbloomberg.ca/marijuana`, which has excellent articles and statistics on publicly listed Canadian (and other) cannabis companies.

As with any emerging industry, the cannabis stock market has been volatile. Investors still trying to find their way in the weed sector are on pins and needles when it comes to bad news and become euphoric when good news surfaces about the industry or a specific company. This market's indexes, charted over a five-year period, look like a scary roller coaster. Be sure that you have the stomach and risk tolerance to play in this space, and diversify your holdings.

The marijuana stock market currently consists of several micro cap players with very small market share. Most of these small fish are pretenders that are not large enough to trade on the main Canadian and U.S. exchanges and instead trade on over-the-counter exchanges or are backed by lesser-known venture capital funds. Be careful here. You can be taken for a ride. Pump-and-dump stock schemes abound in any emerging industry as owners and managers of unscrupulous companies get a listing, pump up the stock with fake news, and sell off their own insider shares.

Future indicators

The basic infrastructure — access to financial markets, the capability to produce marijuana, and lots of smart visionaries with sound business plans — is now in place, and the ecosystem is thriving. Now that cannabis is legal in Canada, other indicators of growth to watch for include new listings of Canadian cannabis companies on major U.S. exchanges such as the New York Stock Exchange (NYSE) or NASDAQ. Companies such as Tilray, Organigram, Cronos, and Valens also trade on major U.S. exchanges, such as the NASDAQ and NYSE, which is good because these exchanges have better exposure and both have a certain cachet that will lend credibility to the sector and the company that is listed.

What other countries do is critical. Look for developments in Italy, Sweden, and of course the U.S. to see if their markets will further open up the domestic as well as the foreign supply of medical and legal marijuana. And find out how many U.S. companies are seeking listings on Canadian exchanges. If banks support the industry, that's another great sign that the sector will continue to thrive due to added financial liquidity. At the time of this writing, U.S. banks cannot transact cannabis business. Perhaps one day soon, one of the multiple attempts at passing the SAFE (Secure and Fair Enforcement) Banking Act in the U.S. will be successful.

Although U.S. laws and Food and Drug Administration regulations are still in a state of flux, one has to ask if our neighbors to the south represent the next big opportunity and super-catalyst. If so, Canadian suppliers are uniquely poised to capitalize because Canada is one of only two major countries — the other is the Netherlands — that currently exports cannabis, to well over 25 other countries. It also helps the future of this sector that the number of companies that have been authorized by Health Canada to produce medicinal marijuana across the country has been steadily increasing.

Legal, regulatory, and other risk factors

This chapter has pointed out the legal and regulatory context of not just the marijuana issue but also how it affects stock investing in this sector. So it stands to reason that the top risks will include legal, regulatory, competitive, financial, and political risks.

You'll have no trouble finding companies with sound business strategies to legally grow and distribute cannabis and then, based on those plans, find financing and a stock listing. The operators often know the business and what they're doing. Although those operating and financial areas represent risks you need to monitor, they're not primary risks. The big risks are as follows:

- Cannabis companies sell to a limited and highly regulated market, making product demand and business expansion to meet demand uncertain.
- The Canadian government's legalization of recreational cannabis is obviously a huge opportunity for this sector as a whole. However, the easing of laws works the other way in the eyes of individual licensed producers and some dispensaries, who will expect to lose market share because some benefit from a more regulated market. We see this happening now with too many dispensaries tightly concentrated in neighbourhood clusters. Competition is fierce and unsustainable.
- New medical marijuana producers and other companies servicing the pot ecosystem have a low entry barrier, although getting a licence to produce is still a big initial hurdle. Even so, many publicly traded cannabis

companies exist, and that number is growing by the month.

- Lots of licenced producers of cannabis grew too fast and furiously on the backs of high debt loads. Many face insolvency as costly interest and debt maturities loom, at the same time that the local or national market may be facing oversupply due to overproduction. The ticker symbols of those gems should include a skull and crossbones or a toxic substance symbol.
- Big Tobacco and Big Pharma are poised to steal customers from pioneering pot firms, siphoning market share and stealing outsized potential gains that would have otherwise gone to the true innovators and investor risk takers.
- The owner-managers of a lot of pot companies, which may have started as small outfits run by great entrepreneurs, obtained easy money and went public too quickly. The problem with many such companies is that their top managers may lack basic governance, financial stewardship, and regulatory and ethical compliance acumen. Be wary of rookie managers.
- Cross-province and cross-state trade regulations would make the head of Perry Mason spin! The legal and logistical complexities are enormous. Where complexity lives, risk thrives.

- Some cannabis stocks sport lofty market capitalizations in the context of existing sales and sometimes unwarranted speculative appeal. They'll need revenue growth to justify current stock prices, let alone move higher.

TIP

Government can definitely get in the way of recreational marijuana production, sale, and use. Political interference on hot button issues like this can and ought to be expected. The issue is the nature and extent of the meddling. Although unlikely to happen soon in Canada given the recent legalization, there is still some residual risk. This risk particularly exposes companies with U.S. assets in that those very assets may be seized at any time by U.S. authorities.

TIP

The Toronto Stock Exchange is keeping a watchful eye on listed Canadian cannabis companies holding U.S. marijuana assets and wants to ensure that the firms are complying with U.S. regulations. That exposes both the listing status of companies listed on the TSX as well as the underlying assets themselves. Marijuana companies with 100 percent of their operations and assets in Canada are likely a much safer investment.

Micro cap cannabis stock evaluation

When evaluating a marijuana stock, micro cap or otherwise, consider the extent to which the company can lay claim to the following favorable factors:

- Reasonable market valuation
- Broad and effective sales and marketing
- Product backing by top consumer retail channels such as pharmacies and liquor stores
- State-of-the-art cultivation facilities
- Low growing costs and high efficiencies
- High-quality core and ancillary products
- Competitive pricing for similar products
- Hedging strategy via permits to sell cannabis to foreign markets exists
- Profitability and cash generation evident
- Minimal exposure to changes in U.S. legislation
- Strong base in high-quality medicinal marijuana
- Sells extracts and cannabis oils that yield high profit margins

Highly speculative pot-related stocks

Some biotech firms are developing cannabinoid drugs which, if they pass clinical trials, could be strong sellers in treating neurological and other disorders. The risk here is that the shares of these firms may have already been hyped to the skies on the dicey prospect that their products under development will pan out. Tread carefully here.

Low-risk pot-related stocks

Consider investing indirectly in low-risk pot-related stocks. Scotts Miracle-Gro is a $5 billion (sales) market leader in the North American lawn-care and garden business. A significant upside for the firm is the specialized soil and plant nutrients it sells to a burgeoning marijuana industry.

Constellation Brands, another blue chip, anchored by its popular Corona beer and Robert Mondavi wines, is a safe play on marijuana with its stake in riskier Canopy Growth.

And by way of subsidiary, Shoppers Drug Mart, Loblaw Cos. Ltd. is angling to be a major pot retailer with its 2,400 or so stores across Canada. Shoppers has already signed up both Tilray and MedReleaf as marijuana suppliers.

TIP

In addition to investing in stocks of companies such as these, consider ETFs. Horizons ETF Management inaugurated the Horizons Medical Marijuana Life Sciences (TSX:HMMJ) on the Toronto Stock Exchange, with many marijuana stocks included in the fund as of now. Flip to Chapter 7 for an introduction to ETFs.

Cannabis companies that have a brand strategy and leverage industry data to fully understand their target consumer will capture disproportionate market share in the world of Cannabis 3.0.

The most important tip is saved for last. Because no one knows which companies will win during the early stages of an emerging new industry, you must pay attention to accounting, which is covered in Chapter 5. Stay clear of debt-ridden companies that do not show revenue growth and at least some hope and promise of positive cash flow and margins. Yes, accounting may be boring, but you will appreciate it when it saves you from losses!

7

Investing in Canadian Exchange-Traded Funds

When it comes to stock investing, you can do it in more than one way. Buying stocks directly is good; sometimes, buying stocks indirectly is equally good (or even better) — especially if you're risk averse. Buying a great stock is every stock investor's dream, but sometimes you face investing environments that make finding a winning stock a hazardous pursuit. Prudent stock investors should consider adding Canadian and U.S. exchange-traded funds (ETFs) to their wealth-building arsenal.

You're first introduced to ETFs in Chapter 1, which discusses equities and the age appropriateness of ETFs at various stages of life. By way of reminder, an *exchange-traded fund (ETF)* is basically a mutual fund that invests in a fixed basket of securities but with a few twists and a lot of benefits.

This chapter shows you how ETFs are similar to (and different from) mutual funds, provides some pointers on picking ETFs, and notes the fundamentals of stock indexes (which are connected to ETFs).

Exchange-Traded Funds Compared to Mutual Funds

For many folks and for many years, the only choice besides investing directly in stocks was to invest indirectly through mutual funds. After all, why buy a single stock for roughly the same few thousand dollars that you can buy a mutual fund for and get benefits such as professional management and diversification?

For small investors, mutual fund investing isn't a bad way to go. Investors participate by pooling their money with others and get professional, convenient money management. But mutual funds have their downsides too. Many, in fact. Mutual fund fees, which include management fees and sales charges (referred to as *loads*), eat into gains, and investors have no choice about investments in a mutual fund. Whatever the fund manager buys, sells, or holds on to is pretty much what the investors in the fund have to tolerate. Investment choice is limited to either being in the fund or being out.

But now, with ETFs, investors have greater choices of fund themes than ever, a scenario that sets the stage for the inevitable comparison between mutual funds and ETFs. The following sections go over the differences and similarities between ETFs and mutual funds.

The differences

Simply stated, in a mutual fund, securities such as stocks and bonds are constantly bought, sold, and held (in other words, the fund is actively managed by a third-party portfolio manager). An ETF holds similar securities, but the portfolio typically isn't actively managed. Instead, an ETF usually holds a fixed basket of securities that may reflect an index or a particular industry or sector (see Chapter 6). An *index* is a method of measuring the value of a segment of the general stock market. It's a tool used by money managers and investors to compare the performance of a particular stock to a widely accepted standard; see the later section "The Basics of Indexes" for more.

For example, an ETF that tries to reflect the S&P/TSX 60 will attempt to hold a securities portfolio that mirrors the composition of the S&P/TSX 60 Index as closely as possible. Here's another example: A water utility's EFT may hold the top 15 or 20 publicly held water companies. (You get the picture.)

Where ETFs are markedly different from mutual funds (and where they're really advantageous) is that they can be bought and sold like stocks. In addition, you can do with ETFs what you can generally do with stocks (but can't usually do with mutual funds): You can buy in share allotments, such as 1, 50, or 100 shares more. Mutual funds, on the other hand, are usually bought in dollar amounts, such as 1,000 or 5,000 dollars' worth. The dollar amount you can initially invest is set by the manager of the individual mutual fund.

Here are some other advantages of ETFs: You can put various buy/sell brokerage orders on ETFs, and many ETFs are optionable (meaning you may be able to buy/sell put and call options on them). Mutual funds typically aren't optionable.

In addition, many ETFs are marginable (meaning that you can borrow against them with some limitations in your brokerage account). Mutual funds usually aren't marginable in Canada or the United States (although it is possible if they're within the confines of a stock brokerage account).

Sometimes an investor can readily see the great potential of a given industry or sector but is hard-pressed to get that single really good stock that can take advantage of the profit possibilities of that particular segment of the market. The great thing about an ETF is that you can make that higher level and thematic investment choice very easily, knowing that if you're unsure about it, you can put in place strategies that protect you from the downside (such as stop-loss orders or trailing stops). That way, you can sleep easier.

The similarities

Even though ETFs and mutual funds have some major differences, they do share a few similarities:

- First and foremost, ETFs and mutual funds (MFs) are similar in that they aren't direct investments; they're conduits of investing, acting like a connection between the investor and the investments.
- Both ETFs and MFs basically pool the money of investors and the pool becomes the "fund," which in turn invests in a portfolio, or basket, of investments.
- Both ETFs and MFs offer the great advantage of diversification (although they accomplish it in different ways).
- Investors don't have any choice about what makes up the portfolio of either the ETF or the MF. The ETF has a fixed basket of securities (the money manager overseeing the portfolio makes those choices), and, of course, investors can't control the choices made in a mutual fund.

TIP

For those investors who want more active assistance in making choices and running a portfolio, mutual funds may be the way to go. For those who are more comfortable making their own choices in terms of the particular index or industry and sector they want to invest in, an exchange-traded fund is a much better venue.

How to Choose an Exchange-Traded Fund

Buying a stock is an investment in a particular company, but an ETF is an opportunity to invest in a block of stocks. In the same way a few mouse clicks can buy you a stock at a stock brokerage website, those same clicks can buy you virtually an entire industry or sector (or at least the top-tier stocks).

For investors who are comfortable with their own choices and do their due diligence, buying a winning stock is a better (albeit more aggressive) way to go. For those investors who want to make their own choices but aren't that confident about picking winning stocks, getting an ETF is definitely a better way to go.

You had to figure that choosing an ETF wasn't going to be a coin flip. You should be aware of certain considerations, some of which are tied more to your personal outlook and preferences than to the underlying portfolio of the ETF. You get the info you need on bullish and bearish ETFs in the following sections.

TIP Picking a winning industry or sector is easier than finding a great company to invest in. Therefore, ETF investing goes hand in hand with the guidance offered in Chapter 6.

Main types of ETFs

You may wake up one day and say, "I think the stock market or a special segment of it will do very well going forward from today," and that's just fine if you think so. Maybe your research on the general economy, financial outlook, and political considerations make you feel happier than a starving man on a cruise ship. But you just don't know (or don't care to research) which stocks would best benefit from the good market moves yet to come. No problem. That's because the following sections cover the primary types of ETFs you can choose from. ETFs represent one of the best examples of what is often referred to as *story investing*.

Major market equity index ETFs

Why not invest in ETFs that mirror a general *major market index* such as the U.S. S&P 500 or Canadian S&P/TSX 60? This type of index ETF tracks the overall market. Other index ETFs track a specific subset of the overall market, such as small capitalization stocks or large capitalization stocks. Subset indexes also exist for sectors such as technology, oil and gas, and consumer goods. The slicing and dicing can go further — much further, in fact, as each year passes and the ETF industry continues to grow.

TIP: Index ETFs typically include equities. The equities may be from Canada, the United States, elsewhere in North America, or they may be global or international in scope. Perhaps the ETF is a combination of all of the above. The bottom line is *anything goes*, so don't worry too much about the categories. What's important is *what* the ETF contains by way of underlying securities, and the trends and stories those stocks and other securities tell.

An index-based ETF tries to earn the return of the market or subset of the market that it seeks to mimic, less the fees. American ETFs such as SPY construct their portfolios to track the composition of the S&P 500 as closely as possible. Canadian ETFs, such as the Horizons AlphaPro Managed S&P/TSX 60, ETF track component stocks within the S&P/TSX 60 Index. As they say, why try to beat the market when you can match it? It's a great way to go when the market is having a good rally. (See the later section "The Basics of Indexes.")

When the S&P 500 and the S&P/TSX 60 were battered over a decade ago during the Great Recession, the respective U.S. and Canadian ETFs, of course, mirrored that performance and hit bottom in early 2009. But from that moment on and well into the time of the writing of this book, the S&P 500 (and the ETFs that tracked it such as the iShares Core S&P 500 ETF) did really well. The ETFs that tracked the S&P/TSX 60 also did reasonably well during this same period. It paid to buck the bearish sentiment of early 2009. Of course it did take some contrarian gumption to do so, but at least you had the benefit of the full S&P 500 stock portfolio, which at least had more diversification than a single stock or a single subsection of the market.

ETFs that include dividend-paying stocks

ETFs don't necessarily have to be tied to a specific industry or sector; they can be tied to a specific type or subcategory of stock. All things being equal, what basic categories of stocks do you think would better weather bad times or suit conservative investors: stocks with no dividends or stocks that pay dividends? (The question answers itself, pretty much like "What tastes better: apple pie or barbed wire?") Although some sectors are known for being good dividend payers, such as utilities (and some good ETFs cover this industry), some ETFs cover stocks that meet a specific criteria.

You can find ETFs that include high-dividend income stocks (typically 4 percent or higher), as well as ETFs that include stocks of companies that don't necessarily pay high dividends but do have a long track record of dividend increases that meet or exceed the rate of inflation.

TIP Given these types of dividend-paying ETFs, it becomes clear what is good for what type of stock investor:

- Stock investors who are currently retired should probably choose the high-dividend stock ETF, along with a bond ETF. Dividend-paying stock ETFs are generally more stable than those stock ETFs that don't pay dividends and, for most Canadians, are important vehicles for generating retirement income.

- Stock investors in pre-retirement (some years away from retirement but clearly planning for it) should probably choose the ETF with the stocks that had a strong record of growing the dividend payout, along with a bond ETF. That way, those same dividend-paying stocks would grow in the short-term and provide better income down the road during retirement.

For more information on dividends, flip to Chapter 3. Chapter 1 covers investing according to age.

Currency ETFs

Currency ETFs are designed to track the performance of a single currency in the foreign exchange market against a benchmark currency or basket of currencies. The way ETFs do this is exotic and beyond the scope of this book. But in short, the ETFs consist of cash deposits, debt instruments denominated in a certain currency, and futures or swap contracts.

Currency markets used to be the playground of experienced traders. However, exchange traded funds kicked open the doors of foreign exchange to Canadian investors. Through a stock market gateway, currency ETFs are used by Canadians who look for exposure to the foreign exchange market, seek diversification, and prefer to transact outside of the complex and cumbersome futures or foreign exchange market.

Fixed-income ETFs

Fixed-income, or *bond, ETFs* are popular with investors who prefer to play it more conservatively, yet still have a bit of upside. This type of ETF may play a good role during times of instability. They are a form of ETF that exclusively invests in fixed-income financial instruments. These holdings can be a portfolio of corporate or government bonds or a combination of the two. They can employ different strategies such as high yield only, and can hold within the ETF long-term or short-term maturity financial instruments. These are called *maturity-themed ETFs.* Take note that the ETF itself has no maturity, and bond ETFs are passively managed. Fixed-income ETFs trade like stock ETFs on a major exchange.

Keep in mind that dividend-paying stocks generally fall within the criteria of "human need" investing because those companies tend to be large and stable, with good cash flows, giving them the ongoing wherewithal to pay good dividends.

TIP

To find out more about ETFs in general and to get more details on the ETFs mentioned (Horizons AlphaPro Managed S&P/TSX 60 ETF, SPY, PBJ, and SH), go to websites such as `www.etf.com` and `www.etfdb.com`. A great way to see whether ETFs exist to fit a theme you have in mind is to simply search for the term in your favorite search engine. For example, if you are intrigued by artificial intelligence, use the search term *ETFs for artificial intelligence.* You'll find news on ETFs such as Horizons Active A.I. Global Equity ETF, which has the cool ticker symbol MIND.

Alternative ETFs related to a strategy

What are alternative ETFs? In a nutshell, an *alternative ETF* is anything that doesn't fit nicely into the equity or other types of ETFs covered so far. Some ETFs cover industries such as food and beverages, water, energy, and other essentials that people will keep buying no matter how good or bad the economy is. Without needing a crystal ball or having an iron-willed contrarian attitude, a stock investor can simply put money into stocks — or in this case, ETFs — tied to human need.

Another type of alternative strategy is to focus on a sector such as commodities. Sub-sectors may include oil and gas, agriculture, sugar, coffee, precious metals, livestock — just about anything. This is where stock investor creativity can pay off.

ETFs may also be thematic by focusing, for instance, on stocks of innovative and growth companies, companies doing business in the middle of a huge trend, or stocks of value companies. Examples of innovation-themed stocks include those from companies in the cannabis, electric vehicle, space exploration, clean energy, and battery development industries. Chapter 3 covers some of the more common approaches to stock investing.

To give you a better sense of the wide array of Canadian ETFs that are out there, check out the following list of ETFs trading on the Canadian stock exchange:

- BMO Agriculture Commodities Index ETF
- BMO Base Metals Commodities Index ETF
- Canadian Small Cap Index Fund
- CDN MSCI World Index Fund
- Claymore Global Monthly Advantaged Dividend ETF
- Claymore Oil Sands Sector ETF
- COMEX Gold ETF
- Horizons Absolute Return Global Currency ETF
- Horizons Canadian Dollar Currency ETF
- Horizons US Dollar Currency ETF
- Horizons U.S. Dollar Bear Plus ETF
- iShares CDN Mid-Cap Index Fund
- iShares CDN MSCI Emerging Markets Index Fund
- iShares CDN REIT Sector Index Fund
- iShares Russell 2000 Index Fund
- S&P/TSX Capped Financials Inverse (bear) ETF

Bearish ETFs

Most ETFs are bullish because they invest in a portfolio of securities that they expect to go up in due course. But some ETFs have a bearish focus. Bearish ETFs (also called short ETFs) maintain a portfolio of securities and strategies that are designed to go the opposite way of the underlying or targeted securities. In other words, this type of ETF goes up when the underlying securities go down (and vice versa). Bearish ETFs employ securities such as put options (and similar derivatives) and employ strategies such as going short.

Take the S&P/TSX 60, for example. If you were bullish on that index, you might choose an ETF such as Horizons AlphaPro Managed S&P/TSX 60. If you were bearish, you could invest in the Horizons BetaPro S&P/TMX 60 Inverse ETF, which seeks investment returns that fully correspond to the inverse of the S&P/TMX 60 Index.

If you were bearish on the US S&P 500 index because of the fiscal cliff and other concerns and wanted to seek gains by betting that it would go down, you could choose an ETF such as the ProShares Short S&P 500 ETF (SH).

You can take two approaches on bearish ETFs:

- **Hoping for a downfall:** If you're speculating on a pending market crash, a bearish ETF is a good consideration. In this approach, you're seeking to make a profit based on your expectations. Folks who aggressively went into bearish ETFs during early or mid 2008 made some spectacular profits during the tumultuous downfall during the Great Recession.

- **Hedging against a downfall:** A more conservative approach is to use bearish ETFs to a more moderate extent, primarily as a form of hedging, whereby the bearish ETF acts like a form of insurance in the unwelcome event of a significant market pullback or crash. You're not really hoping for a crash; you're just trying to protect yourself with a modest form of diversification. In this context, diversification means that you have a mix of both bullish positions and, to a smaller extent, bearish positions.

The Basics of Indexes

For stock investors, ETFs that are bullish or bearish are ultimately tied to major market indexes. You should take a quick look at indexes to better understand them (and the ETFs tied to them).

Whenever you hear the CBC or other media commentary or the scuttlebutt at the local watering hole about "how the market is doing," it typically refers to a market proxy such as an index. You'll usually hear them mention "the Dow" or perhaps the "S&P/TSX 60." There are certainly other major market indexes, and there are many lesser, yet popular, measurements such as the Dow Jones Transportation Average. Indexes and averages tend to be used interchangeably, but they're distinctly different entities of measurement.

Most people use these indexes basically as standards of market performance to see whether they're doing better or worse than a yardstick for comparison. They want to know continually whether their stocks, ETFs, mutual funds, or overall portfolios are performing well.

In Canada, the TSX (`https://tsx.com`) is now Canada's main exchange for the trading of equities. The S&P/TSX 60 Index includes 60 large capitalization stocks for Canadian equity markets. The index is market-capitalization weighted (weighted for company stock market value), weight-adjusted for things such as share float (shares readily available to the public), and balanced across ten industry sectors.

Even though the S&P/TSX 60 Index contains the big guns as its constituent companies, the S&P/TSX Composite Index is the headline benchmark Canadian index, and the one you hear about on the radio the most. It represents about 1,640 companies that make up the index. (See Chapter 3 for more about stock exchanges.)

8

Dealing with Taxes

How much tax does investment income draw? Yup, you guessed it — it depends.

Different forms of income attract different levels of taxation. For example, relative to other types of investment income, interest income draws the most punishing tax. Things get a bit more lenient with dividend income, where the Canada Revenue Agency (CRA) taxes you but may also give you a tax credit to cushion the blow. With capital gains, the CRA hits you with only half a blow — only a fraction of your gains or losses are included in, or deducted from, your income. This chapter explores these tax-related issues.

Interest Income

Interest income is taxable in full in the year in which it's received. No deductions or credits are associated with interest income, other than any small expenses incurred to actually earn interest, such as bank fees. Bank accounts, guaranteed investment certificates (GICs), term deposits, mortgages receivable, and bonds are some of the financial instruments out there that produce interest income.

The CRA wants your interest income so much that, for interest income on compound-interest obligations obtained in 1990 or later, interest has to be reported on an annual accrual basis from the investment's anniversary date. That means you report it as though you have received interest even if you haven't. For example, if you invested in a compound-interest–bearing bond on June 30, 2022 that matures in June 2023, you do not have to include in the 2022 tax year interest that accrued as of December 31, 2022. However, in 2023, you must report interest earned from July 1, 2022 to June 30, 2023. It is best to have interest-bearing bonds that mature after the year-end.

Treasury bills

For Treasury bills (T-bills), the difference between your acquisition cost and the selling price at maturity is interest. A capital gain is realized only if market interest rates drop and the

Treasury bills (now worth more) are sold before maturity. The capital gain equals the selling price less the purchase cost plus accrued interest up to the date of disposition. You may have to report a capital loss if the opposite happens and rates rise.

Indexed securities

Indexed securities are financial instruments that provide interest at a rate below the current market rate. However, the amount payable upon maturity is generally adjusted based on the change in a purchasing power index, such as the Canada Consumer Price Index (CPI). In these circumstances, if there is an upward adjustment, the increase is included in the investor's income as interest. If there is a downward adjustment, the reverse happens and the adjustment is generally deductible by the investor. Your tax slip, normally the T5 slip, provides the detailed amount that needs to be included in your tax return.

Providers of investment vehicles (such as banks that provide GICs) are required by law to send their clients annual information slips (T5 — Statement of Investment Income) reporting interest, dividends, and other forms of investment income. You will also likely receive a T5008 Statement of Securities Transactions from your financial institution. This slip discloses the amount paid or credited to you for securities you sold or redeemed during the year.

TIP: As you can see, some interest-bearing investments, such as T-bills and indexed instruments, have unique reporting methods. Other uniquely treated investments include annuity contracts, investments bought at a discount to face value, stripped bonds, and Canada Savings Bonds. Consider these nuances when making investment and tax-planning decisions; they can have a major effect on your taxes payable. Check out these and other current tax law requirements at the CRA website (`www.canada.ca/en/revenue-agency`).

Canada Savings Bonds (CSBs) are no longer available for purchase as of November 2017. Any bonds you already own are guaranteed and continue to earn interest until maturity or redemption, whichever comes first.

TIP: It's a good idea to keep bonds inside a registered account such as a registered retirement savings plan (RRSP), registered retirement income fund (RRIF), or tax-free savings account (TFSA). Interest is taxed at a high rate, and the bookkeeping, which is a nuisance, is avoided if bonds are inside a registered account.

Dividend Income

Compared to interest income, any eligible dividends you receive from a Canadian corporation are subject to preferential tax rates. Eligible dividends are typically captured automatically on your T5. They are taxed at a lower rate because of the availability of a dividend tax credit. This dividend tax credit is available to you because the corporation has already paid tax on the earnings when it distributed them as dividends to you. In this way, the CRA guards against double taxation.

Dividend income received from foreign companies — before any withholding tax is held back — is taxed at the same full tax rates as interest income. There is no gross-up and dividend tax credit treatment (see the section "Grossed out," later in this chapter). The absence of a dividend tax credit makes sense because the CRA doesn't tax foreign corporations, so there is no double taxation issue in the first place.

Dividends included in your tax return are converted to Canadian dollars, of course. However, a foreign tax credit is available for any foreign taxes that are withheld. So foreign dividends are taxed more like interest instead of like dividends from Canadian companies.

If dividends from Canadian and foreign corporations were received inside your RRSP, tax on this income is deferred. When you finally withdraw money from your RRSP, it will be fully taxable as regular income. That's because inside RRSPs, investment income loses its nature and comes in only one flavour — high-tax vanilla. Inside RRSPs, you also lose the tax advantage of applying the dividend or foreign tax credit.

There are also financial animals called *capital gains dividends,* which are distributions that may come from Canadian mutual funds, exchanged-traded funds (ETFs), and real estate investment trusts (REITs). For REITs, any dividend payments made by the REIT are taxed to the unitholder as ordinary income, unless they're considered qualified dividends, in which case they're taxed as capital gains. Your T5 slip sorts this out for you, so don't worry. For capital gains dividends, just realize that one half of the capital gain distributed will be taxable on your tax return.

TIP

Distributions made by Canadian ETFs can take on many forms as well in the eyes of the CRA. They can be one or a combination of Canadian dividends eligible for dividend tax credit treatment; capital gains (only 50 percent taxable) return of capital (not taxable, but triggers a reduction of the adjusted cost base); other income (100 percent taxable); and foreign income (100 percent taxable). Your T5 usually comes to the rescue and will indicate the split.

Any distributions you receive from foreign ETFs as a Canadian are usually treated as foreign dividends, which are 100 percent taxable. When distributions from U.S. ETFs are categorized as capital gains or return of capital for U.S. taxpayers, they're still fully taxable in the hands of Canadian taxpayers.

Grossed out

If you received dividends from a taxable Canadian corporation, you must gross the dividends up by 38 percent (that is, multiply them by 1.38) and then include that grossed-up amount in your taxable income. Hey, that's not fair. But wait — the federal dividend tax credit mentioned previously (or 15.02 percent of the grossed-up eligible dividend) reduces your federal income tax payable. Provincial tax credits are available, too. Okay, that's better.

Provinces now have their own dividend tax credit, similar to the federal credit. Previously, provincial tax was calculated as a simple percentage of the federal tax after the federal dividend tax credit was applied.

Stock dividends and splits

A *stock dividend* is a dividend that a corporation pays by issuing shares instead of cash. Stock dividends are generally considered to be ordinary taxable dividends and are treated as such. The amount of the dividend you include in taxable income — your share of the increase in paid-up capital — also represents the cost of your new shares for future sales as well as capital gain or loss calculations.

Stock splits — where you get more shares without any change in the total dollar value of those shares — are not taxable. You gained or lost nothing from an economic or a tax standpoint.

TIP

When you get your T3 (Statement of Trust Income Allocations and Designations) or T5 tax slip showing, among other things, your annual dividend income (including any stock dividend values), you'll see that there are boxes that contain both the actual dividends and the taxable amount of dividends paid. Be careful to include only the taxable amount of dividends on your tax return.

Capital Gains and Losses

A *capital gain* occurs when you sell or otherwise dispose of a capital property for more than what you paid for it — technically, the CRA refers to this cost as the *adjusted cost base* because they may sometimes require you to adjust your original cost. However, this chapter keeps things simple and leaves special rules about costs out of the picture for now. Just keep in mind that capital gains are reduced by any disposition costs incurred, such as brokers' commissions.

Unlike ordinary income such as salary or interest, only 50 percent of the capital gain that you make outside your RRSP is included in your taxable income. This is called a taxable capital gain, and this portion of the total capital gain is taxed in the year of the sale. If you suffer a *capital loss* — where your costs exceed your proceeds — the 50 percent allowable portion should first be used to offset any taxable capital gains that may exist in the same year. The allowable capital loss cannot be used to reduce other income except under special circumstances such as death. Any unused allowable capital loss can be carried back up to three years or carried forward indefinitely, but only to reduce any future taxable capital gains.

Keep in mind that just because you didn't receive any proceeds from a sale, that doesn't always mean that you have no capital gain or loss to report. A special scenario can play out when you gift shares or other capital property to family members. In such cases, the CRA may deem you to have received fair-market-value consideration at the time of the gift (or a sale for less than fair market value). The amount of cash actually changing hands is irrelevant to the CRA.

The CRA has certain rules concerning superficial losses. A superficial loss occurs if you execute a transaction (such as a sale or other transfer of investments) that creates a loss while you, or a related person, keep or quickly regain control of the same (or identical) property that created the loss in the first place. The CRA applies the superficial loss provision beginning 30 calendar days before and ending 30 calendar days after the disposition of a property. In other words, no fancy footwork (such as the manipulation of the timing or ownership of losses) is permitted a month before or after the sale.

About the Authors

Andrew Dagys, CPA, CMA, is a best-selling author who has written and co-authored more than a dozen books, mostly about investing, personal finance, and technology. Andrew has contributed columns to major Canadian publications and is also a frequently quoted author in many of Canada's daily news publications, including *The Globe and Mail, National Post,* and *Toronto Star.* He has appeared on several national news broadcasts to offer his insights into the Canadian and global investment landscapes. Andrew considers writing books, in collaboration with talented publishing and editorial partners, to be one of life's most truly amazing experiences.

Andrew enjoys actively serving his community in the not-for-profit sector. He lives in Toronto with his wife, Dawn-Ava, and their three children — Brendan, Megan, and Jordan.

Paul Mladjenovic, CFP, is a certified financial planner practitioner, writer, and public speaker. His business, PM Financial Services, has helped people with financial and business concerns since 1981. In 1985, he achieved his CFP designation. Since 1983, Paul has taught thousands of budding investors through popular national seminars such as "The $50 Wealthbuilder" and "Stock Investing Like a Pro." Paul has been quoted or referenced by many media outlets, including Bloomberg, MarketWatch, Comcast, CNBC, and a variety of financial and business publications and websites. As an author, he has written the books *The Unofficial Guide to Picking Stocks* (Wiley, 2000) and *Zero-Cost Marketing* (Todd Publications, 1995), among others.